foster harris house
cookbook

For Finn

What started as a little project blossomed into a yearlong endeavor involving the help of a number of talented people. First and foremost, my sincere thanks to John Spaulding for his beautiful photography. John came to us as a Foster Harris House guest, became a friend and just happened to be a gifted food photographer. His thoughtful approach and easygoing demeanor made the long hours spent on this project a pleasure. I'd also like to thank R.H. Ballard Art, Rug & Home for the beautiful place settings and accessories, Adrienne and Margaret Brown for their help setting the tables, Tanner Latham for editorial input, Betty Sisk, our in-house "Mom" and all-around lifesaver, Cathy MacPherson for testing recipes, critiquing my food, and for being the best Auntie to Finn, and Jan and Tom MacPherson for raising my sister and me in a loving, cheerful and delicious home. Most importantly, I'd like to thank Diane and Finn for being the two very best parts of my life.

Photographer: John Spaulding
Art Design and Editor: Diane MacPherson

FOSTER HARRIS HOUSE COOKBOOK
Text Copyright © 2008, 2011 by John MacPherson
Photography Copyright © 2008, 2011 by John Spaulding
All rights reserved.

Published by
One Tree Island, LLC
P.O. Box 333, Washington, VA 22747 U.S.A.
(540) 675-3757
www.fosterharris.com

ISBN: 978-0-578-00108-1

Printed in Korea by Graphics International

foster harris house

cookbook

john macpherson

photography by john spaulding
edited by diane macpherson

contents

Introduction

Food -- more precisely, the act of planning, shopping, preparing, cooking, and eating -- has been a central part of my family's life since well before I was born. My Mom and Dad grew up in Boston, each with an Italian mother. Mom went to school in the North End, a neighborhood anchored by *Modern Pastry, Galleria Umberto* and *Café Vittoria*. These restaurants still celebrate the act of slowing down in the middle of the day to savor a tender calzone, a rich espresso and a crispy, sweet cannoli.

John, with his sister Cathy and mother Jan, enjoying a New England favorite

That's why I grew up thinking it was perfectly normal to celebrate Thanksgiving with a traditional turkey dinner as well as a full compliment of Italian specialties: lasagna, meatballs, bracciole, and squid in gravy. There'd be enough to feed a small army, because, as Mom would say, "you never knew who might drop by." To this day, my sister Cathy and I are probably the only kids to bring leftover squid to school for lunch!

So it's no surprise that cooking is a big part of our lives here at the Foster Harris House. Whether we're serving breakfast to our guests, eating a simple family meal, or hosting an impromptu dinner with neighbors to use up a bumper crop of tomatoes, we see every meal as a celebration.

One of the greatest joys in my life is preparing and sharing a meal with family and friends. I hope you'll enjoy sharing these recipes with yours.

Cheers!

John

the foster harris house story

In 1899, a woman by the name of Sarah Compton bought a piece of land on the edge of the town of Washington, Virginia. The town had been surveyed exactly 150 years earlier by a teenager named George Washington who would eventually give his name to countless hamlets across the country. But, as lore would have it, this Washington was the first to bear his name and that's why the town's historical markers proclaim it to be "the first Washington of them all."

The Comptons were an established local family prominent in church, community and civil affairs. Sarah's husband, John A. Compton (right) was justice of the peace for many years and his daughter, Ms. Margaret Compton, was a school teacher, justice of the peace after her father's death and registrar of vital statistics for the county.

The Foster Harris House has a long history of accommodating travelers: In the 1950s, Margaret Compton converted the house into a "tourist home." The property was called the Maple Leaf Lodge and the sign hanging in front of the house says, "Rooms and Bath for Tourists."

1899 - 1963

The land that is now home to the Foster Harris House is purchased by Sarah Compton on Jan. 10, 1899. On April 1, 1904, permission is given to Sarah and John Compton to erect a house on the land. They have six children: William, Ida, Charles, Margaret, Ernest, and Floyd. Ownership of house is transferred to Margaret.

The Foster Harris House in the 1950s

She owns the house until she passes away on December 15, 1963.

1964 - 1981

Zorelda A. Updike purchases the property in 1964. On Dec. 18, 1976 she passes away and leaves the property to her daughter, Edna Updike Mello who keeps it until 1981.

1981 - 1992

On Oct. 1, 1981, Danny Patrick Foster and Camille Anne Harris purchase the property from Edna Mellow Updike. They convert the property into a bed and breakfast and own it until 1992.

1992 - 1997

Phyllis Marriott is the proprietor.

1997 - 2002

John and Olivia Byam are the proprietors.

2002 - 2004

Patrick and Rita Corbett are the proprietors.

2004 - present

Diane and John MacPherson are the proprietors.

The Foster Harris House today

a brief photo history

Bed and breakfasts across the U.S. experienced a surge in popularity in the 1980s. People were interested in historic preservation and they wanted the warm, cozy feeling of staying at Grandma's, even if it meant sharing a bathroom with other guests and having the owner's housecat wandering through the rooms. But by the late 1990s, bed and breakfasts were becoming more of a mainstream option for travellers, and properties that were once considered quaint needed to provide more luxurious décor and finer amenities to attract a broader audience.

The Foster Harris House was no exception. While every owner has made improvements to the house to keep up with the times, we're grateful to note that they've all taken great care to preserve its original charm. Here are some photos showing its evolution over the past 25 years:

In 1981, when Patrick Foster and Camille Harris purchased the house, it had fallen into disrepair. As you can see from this photo of Patrick stripping wallpaper from the upstairs foyer, they had to completely renovate the property to make it livable again. Thank you, Patrick and Camille!

The kitchen, circa 1982

The kitchen today

The living room, circa 1982

The living room today

The Compton Room, 1999

The Compton Room today

The Mary Ellen Jenkins Room, 1999

The Mary Ellen Jenkins Room today

our story

People often ask what motivated us to move from Laguna Beach, California to a rural town in Virginia. Laguna Beach is a truly wonderful place to live – pristine beaches, fabulous food and wine, perfect weather year-round – but anyplace can feel like a gilded cage when one's career becomes dissatisfying.

John on Woods Cove Beach in Laguna Beach, CA

When we met in 2001, John ran a fireplace design studio while I worked for a management consulting firm. Although we both loved our jobs for a long time, we had come to the point where we were living for the weekends. As foodies and avid cyclists, we'd spend our free time wine tasting, visiting art galleries, eating out, cooking in, and riding our bikes. John raced his bicycle competitively, so we spent many weekends at his races.

In January of 2004, John had a race in Santa Barbara, so we drove up the coast and stayed at a B&B there. During dinner, we were commiserating about the prospect of returning to work on Monday when John said, "we should open up a bed and breakfast." Well, the idea struck us like a cartoon lightening bolt. We realized that by running a bed and breakfast (and eventually starting the cycling tours we dreamed about) we could incorporate into our day-to-day lives everything we truly enjoyed.

John cycling up Alpe d'Huez in the Central French Alps

We loved living in California and we like the climate in wine growing regions, so we started looking for bed and breakfasts in Napa Valley. Nothing quite suited us and, since we knew we wanted to have a baby, we began to consider how difficult it would be for our families (all living on the East Coast) to visit. Some friends suggested we look in Virginia. It wasn't even on the radar for us, but we valued their opinion, so we came out for a visit.

We took a whirlwind tour of Virginia, driving over 1000 miles in five days. All the places we visited were beautiful, but when we came to Rappahannock County, we were awestruck. The roads are perfect for cycling, there are vineyards, art galleries and great places to eat. Who would imagine

that *The Inn at Little Washington*, one of the finest restaurants in the world, would be nestled in this tiny village?

We contacted our real estate agent and asked him to call all of the inns in this area to see if anyone was willing to sell. Happily, the owners of the Foster Harris House had been considering the idea, so the timing was right. We took ownership of the Foster Harris House in September of 2004 and haven't felt as if we've worked a day since then.

In June of 2005, we launched our cycling touring business, Tour d'Epicure. It's been growing as more people discover that the countryside is even more breathtaking from the seat of a bicycle and how the region's fine cuisine transports one to even greater heights of pleasure after a day of vigorous activity.

In January 2006, our son Finn was born. We don't take for granted our ability to equally share the awesome responsibility of raising a child and the joy of witnessing his day-to-day discoveries together.

Diane and John hold a four-day-old Finn Alexander MacPherson

Many of our guests have asked us if we planned to publish a cookbook and, as you can see, there's never a dull moment here at the Foster Harris House. Between our two businesses and raising a son, it's been tough to find the time to undertake such a project. Yet, somehow, when something is close to your heart, it eventually makes its way to the front burner.

- Diane MacPherson

your story

Tens of thousands of guests have passed through the doors of the Foster Harris House since it became a bed and breakfast in the early 1980s. People from all over the world have turned the brass knob on the front door, smoothed the century-old railing as they climbed the stairs, and retreated to rooms overlooking the ancient foothills of the Blue Ridge Mountains.

People come to breathe in the fresh mountain air, to rejuvenate when work has beaten them up a little, to rediscover each other when they're finally able to get a sitter for the weekend. People come to propose marriage, to finish writing novels, to re-evaluate priorities, to honor milestones, and to savor precious moments between tours of duty.

Our guests may have different reasons for getting away, but their convergence in this region -- and ours, for that matter -- is no coincidence: we found the Foster Harris House because we all love food. Thanks in great part to *The Inn at Little Washington* and the flourishing local farms and wineries, our region has become known as a culinary destination.

What a joy it is for us to be among people who love food as much as we do. We never grow tired of hearing our guests share their dinner experiences: the crusty breads with pecans and sea salt, succulent short ribs, decadent foie gras... During breakfast, they share cooking techniques, compare stories about exotic food experiences in the farthest corners of the earth and reveal undiscovered food havens on side streets of their home towns. Sure, they talk about other things, but food is the most common theme among our guests.

This cookbook wouldn't exist if it weren't for you, so we've peppered these pages with your musing about this gastronomic passion that connects us all.

getting started

While cooking is a very personal endeavor and the way you go about it is completely up to you, there are a few things that will make using this book a bit easier and give you the best results:

ingredients

- salt is coarse Kosher
- pepper is fresh ground
- olive oil is extra virgin
- butter is unsalted
- flour is all-purpose
- eggs are extra large grade A

kitchen tools

You don't need anything fancy, but the following tools makes prepping ingredients much more pleasant:

- good quality, sharp, carbon steel chef's knife
- paring knife
- oven-safe Teflon pan
- good quality stainless steel sauté pan
- 2-quart stock pot
- 16 – 24 quart stock pot with riveted handles
- set of biscuit cutters
- chinoise or China cap (for the smoothest sauces)
- food processor
- parchment paper
- large cast iron skillet and griddle
- off-set spatula
- stick (immersion) blender

the oven

Oven temperatures are in Fahrenheit and baking times are for a convection oven. If you have a conventional oven, you'll need to increase the baking temperature by 25° and baking time by 25%. To keep food warm, the oven should be set for 180°.

In the end, all you really need is a love of food. Now let's cook something up!

breakfast

Ideas for breakfast at the Foster Harris House emerged long before we took ownership of the inn. We thought about what we'd serve and how we'd present it. I made egg dishes a thousand ways, baked soufflés, fried bacon and sausage and griddled pancakes. My wife Diane served as taste tester and resident reviewer.

We thought about making breakfast available all morning, or maybe continental style or self serve. But, in the end, we really wanted it to be a proper meal with a start, middle and end. We didn't want it to be stuffy or formal. I decided to take the standard breakfast fare and change it up a bit. Elevate bacon and eggs to something fun and unexpected. Why not serve smaller courses instead of one full plate? We wanted breakfast to be a feast for the eyes as well as the stomach. What has evolved over the four short years we've been taking care of this great old house is a bunch of recipes that are fun to make, delicious to eat and beautiful on the plate.

Wake everyone up with the smell of fresh brewed coffee and the scent of ginger scones. Breakfast is the most important meal of the day, after all.

Every morning, Diane prepares either this fruit parfait or the citrus salad with ginger yogurt as a first course for breakfast.

diane's fruit parfait

10 large strawberries

1 large mango

1 or 2 ripe kiwi

½ pint blueberries

18 ounces Yoplait vanilla custard yogurt

¼ cup granola

mint sprigs for garnish

Trim the green leaves off the strawberries. Cut the strawberries vertically into 16 - 24 thin slices and lay out on a cutting board. Dice the remaining pieces and place in medium bowl. Peel mango and slice off both sides as close to the pit as possible. Cut the remaining mango off pit. Slice the 2 halves of the mango lengthwise into thin crescent shapes and lay out on the cutting board. Dice any extra pieces and place into bowl. Peel kiwi, cutting 8 thin, round discs and lay out on the cutting board. Dice the remaining kiwi and place into bowl. Set aside 8 blueberries for garnish and add the rest to the bowl, stirring gently to combine.

In a decorative 6-ounce glass, place a tablespoon of yogurt, then a tablespoon of the fruit mixture. Arrange the sliced fruit around the edge of the glass, then add another tablespoon of diced fruit. Top with a tablespoon of yogurt, a blueberry and some granola. Garnish with a sprig of mint. Serves 8

citrus salad with ginger yogurt

1 pink grapefruit, peeled

2 large tangerines or tangelos, peeled

3 navel oranges

½ cup dried cranberries, plus extra for garnish

2 tablespoons honey

¼ teaspoon ground cinnamon

1 16-ounce container vanilla yogurt, drained

⅓ cup minced crystallized ginger

¼ cup golden brown sugar

mint sprig for garnish

Break grapefruit and tangerines into sections. Cut grapefruit sections into thirds; cut tangerine sections in half. Transfer grapefruit, tangerines, and all juices to a large bowl. Using a small sharp knife, cut all peel and white pith from oranges. Slice oranges into ¼-inch-thick rounds, then cut slices into quarters. Add oranges and all juices to same bowl. Mix in ½ cup dried cranberries, honey, and cinnamon. Cover and refrigerate at least 1 hour.

In a small bowl, mix together yogurt and ginger. Fruit and yogurt can be prepared a day ahead, covered separately and refrigerated. To serve, spoon fruit into decorative 6-ounce glasses and top with a spoonful of the ginger yogurt. Sprinkle with brown sugar and dried cranberries. Serves 8

the unassuming egg

Most folks don't give a minute's thought to an egg before cracking it into a pan or whipping it into a batter, but the humble egg is an amazing, self-contained powerhouse food. The perfect blend of fat, protein and nutrients, it can be separated into its two components -- the yolk and the white -- one rich with fat, the other light with protein. The shell can even be used to clarify broth or consommé.

Needless to say, we use a fair number of eggs at the *Foster Harris House*. Fried, poached, scrambled, whipped into a soufflé; we make eggs literally dozens of ways. For frying, I use olive oil, because it won't burn like butter. I use butter for scrambled eggs and omelets, because the temperature is lower and the butter accentuates the richness of the eggs. Poached eggs should have a little jiggle to them and scrambled should be moist and shiny. A well-prepared egg is just plain delicious!

fried eggs

2 large, very fresh eggs
2 tablespoons olive oil
salt and pepper

Heat oil in a large non-stick pan over medium-high heat. When oil is hot, carefully crack each egg into pan. Cook undisturbed for 2 minutes. If you want firmer yolks, cover the pan for another minute. When the eggs are done to your liking, place them on a warm plate, season with salt and pepper and serve immediately. Serves 2

cooking fiasco #1

"My biggest cooking fiasco? Making toast! Prior to moving from Ft. Lewis, Washington to the D.C. area, my husband and I had a brief stay at the guesthouse on the Ft. Lewis military installation. The lodging rules were very strict: No cooking of any kind in the guest rooms. Nonetheless, I just happened to have a toaster amongst my collection of necessities, it was 6:00 am, I was hungry, and anyone can make toast, right? Much to my horror, the toast began to burn and a thick, black smoke billowed from the coils, causing the fire alarm to pierce through the still of the morning. As I stood alongside the 200-plus guests, all in their pajamas, half-asleep kids in tow, I still believed I was safe from discovery until the entire fire crew, decked out in full fire-fighting regalia, approached and informed me that the alarm was triggered from my room, due to the presence and subsequent use of an illegal toaster. In retrospect, remaining in the room and passing out from smoke inhalation would've been a far wiser choice . . ."

– Marlene Champagne, Alexandria, VA

For optimum fluffiness, a properly "scrambled" egg is actually gently folded.

scrambled eggs

6 large, very fresh eggs
¼ cup half and half
4 tablespoons butter
salt and fresh ground pepper

Warm serving plate in 180° oven. In a medium bowl, add eggs and half and half, whisking to combine. Heat butter in a large non-stick pan over medium-high heat. When butter has melted, add egg mixture and shake pan until eggs start to set. Fold eggs gently from the inside of the pan to the outside, taking care not to scramble them too much. When the eggs are just barely set, place them on the warm plate, season with salt and pepper and serve immediately. Serves 6

There's no need to fear poaching an egg and no need for special pans either.

perfectly simple poached eggs

6 large, very fresh eggs

2 tablespoons white vinegar

1 tablespoon salt

Warm a large, flat plate in a 180° oven. Fill a large deep pan with water to within an inch of the top. Add the vinegar and salt and bring to a very light simmer. The bubbles in the water should be visible at the bottom but barely breaking on the surface of the water. Crack an egg into a small bowl and then gently slide the egg into the water. Repeat with the remaining eggs.

Poach for about 3 minutes or until the eggs are set to your liking. Test the eggs by sliding a rubber spatula underneath each one and check the amount of jiggle. You want the eggs to move a bit without being set firm. Remove each egg with a slotted spoon in the order it was added. Trim rough edges from each egg with the edge of the spatula.

Place the eggs on the warm plate and serve immediately. The eggs can also be held for a bit by covering them with foil and placing in a warm oven at 180°. Makes 6 eggs

No one is able to resist these light, buttery scones. The key to great scones is keeping everything cold. Put the cutting board, mixing bowls and pastry blender in the fridge before starting. After cutting the butter into the dry ingredients, put the bowl back into the fridge for a few minutes.

ginger scones

2 cups all-purpose flour

⅓ cup sugar

1 tablespoon baking powder

½ teaspoon salt

8 tablespoons very cold unsalted butter

¾ cup chopped candied ginger

1 egg, lightly beaten

½ cup heavy cream, plus more for brushing

raw sugar for dusting

Preheat oven to 425°. Place ungreased baking sheet in freezer. Place flour, sugar, baking powder and salt in a cold, large mixing bowl and whisk to combine. Cut in the butter with a pastry blender until pea-sized pieces are left. Stir in ginger. Set aside in the fridge.

In a separate bowl whisk together egg and cream. Pour egg mixture into dry ingredients and mix just until incorporated. Knead a few times in the bowl to bring the dough together. Turn the dough out onto a cold, floured surface and form into a flat disc about ¾-inch thick. Cut out 2-inch rounds with a biscuit cutter and place on a cold, ungreased baking sheet 1½ inches apart. Brush tops with cream and dust with raw sugar. Bake for 10-12 minutes until just golden brown. Makes 12-18 scones

The smell of fresh baked scones wafts through the house every morning as we prepare breakfast for our guests. To avoid this daily temptation, we deliver any extras to our neighbor immediately after breakfast, and keep this low-carbohydrate variety on hand to satisfy the craving.

star anise low-carb scones

2 cups soy flour

⅓ cup Splenda

1 tablespoon baking powder

½ teaspoon salt

8 tablespoons very cold unsalted butter

2 teaspoons ground star anise

2 teaspoons grated lemon zest

1 egg, lightly beaten

½ cup heavy cream, plus more for brushing

1 tablespoon raw sugar (optional)

Preheat oven to 425°. Place ungreased baking sheet in freezer. Place flour, Splenda, baking powder and salt in a cold, large mixing bowl and whisk to combine. Cut in the butter with a pastry blender until pea-sized pieces are left. Stir in anise and zest. Set aside in the fridge.

Whisk together egg and cream. Pour egg mixture into dry ingredients and mix just until incorporated. Knead a few times in the bowl to bring the dough together then turn the dough out onto a cold, floured surface and form into a flat disc about ¾-inch thick. Cut out 2-inch rounds with a biscuit cutter and place on cold, ungreased baking sheet 1½ inches apart. Brush tops with cream and, if you're willing to add a few carbs for the sake of a sparkle and crunch, sprinkle with raw sugar. Bake for 10–12 minutes until just golden brown. Makes 12-18 scones

nutrition facts

serving size: 1 scone   servings per recipe: 16
calories: 126   carbohydrates: 6g   fiber: 2g   protein: 6g   fat: 9g

cutting decorative leaves

- To cut a shape out of pastry dough, use a very sharp small-blade knife, such as an Exacto knife.

- The dough should be cold enough to hold its shape, but not frozen. If the dough gets too warm, simple place it in the freezer for a few minutes.

- After cutting out the leaf shapes, score the tops to look like veins.

- Finish your pastry creation with a brush of egg wash and bake according to the recipe

One of our most popular entrees, this dish awakens the taste buds with sweet, salty, tangy, creamy, flaky goodness. It's best to make the bacon the night before and reheat it in a warm oven for 30 minutes before serving.

puff pastry with poached egg and avocado salsa

1 sheet puff pastry

2 tablespoons red onion, finely diced

¼ cup chopped cilantro

2 ripe heirloom tomatoes, chopped

½ cup mango, diced

2 ripe avocados, diced

juice of 1 lime

6 poached eggs (page 30)

6 pieces Paradise Bacon (page 38)

chipotle cream sauce (page 163)

diced red pepper for garnish

Heat oven to 400°. Cut puff pastry into six 2x2-inch squares and place on parchment-lined baking sheet. Cut out 6 decorative leaves and place on sheet. Bake pastry until puffed and golden brown, about 13 minutes. Set aside.

For salsa, place onion, cilantro, tomatoes, mango, avocado and lime juice in a mixing bowl and stir to combine. Season to taste with salt. To prevent oxidation, cover with plastic wrap pressed directly on top of salsa and refrigerate until ready to use. Poach eggs according to recipe on page 30 and hold covered in a warm oven until ready to assemble dish.

To plate this dish, dab center of plate with chipotle cream sauce to hold the puff pastry in place. Put puff pastry square in center of plate and top with poached egg. Place a piece of bacon and ¼ cup of salsa on either side. Drizzle egg with chipotle cream, top with a pastry leaf and garnish with red pepper. Serves 6

This bacon is a guest favorite at the Foster Harris House. We make it with either raspberry chipotle sauce or mango chutney, both of which are fantastic.

paradise bacon

½ cup raspberry chipotle sauce (page 167) or mango chutney (page 162)

12 thick slices (about ¾ pound) hickory smoked bacon

Preheat oven to 375°. Arrange bacon in a single layer on a baking rack placed on a baking sheet lined with foil or parchment. Bake for 15 minutes until the bacon begins to look opaque and the fat begins to render. Remove from oven and blot top of bacon with paper towels to dry.

Brush top of bacon with the sauce, return to oven and bake for an additional 12-15 minutes, until browned. Keep an eye on the bacon as it can burn quickly. The bacon will be chewy and crunchy, but stays short of dry and crisp. Cool, then refrigerate flat (use parchment paper between layers if stacking).

To hold the bacon in a cylindrical shape, wrap it around a 1-inch dowel and roll in parchment paper before reheating it in a 180° oven. Makes 12 slices

This recipe works for dinner as well as breakfast and is a great way to use day-old bread.

poached eggs on toast with sautéed spinach and crispy prosciutto

1 cup plus 4 tablespoons olive oil

2 garlic cloves, peeled, crushed

1 tablespoon chopped, fresh thyme

1 teaspoon dried, crushed red pepper

salt and pepper to taste

4 slices Italian bread, 1-inch thick

8 very thin slices of prosciutto, julienned

2 tablespoons minced shallot

1 10-ounce bag fresh baby spinach

4 poached eggs (page 30)

shaved Parmesan cheese

Preheat oven to 400°. Combine 1 cup olive oil, garlic, thyme and red pepper in small saucepan. Cook over medium heat for 2 minutes to infuse oil. Remove from heat and season mixture to taste with salt and pepper. Brush bread slices all over with olive oil mixture and bake until bread is golden brown, about 8 minutes. Set bread aside and reduce oven temperature to 180°. Prepare poached eggs, cover and keep warm.

Heat 2 tablespoons olive oil in large skillet over medium-high heat and cook the julienned prosciutto until crisp. Transfer to paper towels to drain. To cook spinach, heat remaining 2 tablespoons olive oil in large pan over medium heat. Add shallot and sauté for 2 minutes, then add spinach and stir until just wilted. Remove from heat. Top bread slices with spinach and place in oven until heated through, about 5 minutes.

Serve topped with a poached egg, prosciutto, and shaved Parmesan. Serves 4

wild mushroom, spinach and gruyère frittata

4 tablespoons butter, divided

1 shallot minced

2 cups coarse chopped wild mushrooms (chanterelle, morel, shiitake, etc...)

16 large eggs

½ cup whole milk

½ cup heavy cream

⅓ cup cream cheese

2 cups grated Gruyère cheese

½ cup cooked spinach, squeezed dry and chopped

½ teaspoon salt

¼ teaspoon fresh ground pepper

10 potato latke (page 135)

10 Gruyère chips (page 76)

basil Hollandaise (page 163)

parsley sprigs for garnish

Heat oven to 350°. Heat 2 tablespoons butter over medium heat in a large ovenproof non-stick pan. Add shallot and cook for 1 minute. Add mushrooms and cook until moisture has evaporated and they start to brown, about 8 minutes. Season to taste with salt and pepper. Remove to a clean bowl and set aside. Wipe pan clean.

Whisk eggs, milk and cream in a large bowl until well blended. Add cream cheese to the egg mixture by pinching off little bits the size of a dime, then dropping them in. Add Gruyère, mushrooms, spinach, salt and pepper and stir to combine.

Heat the same pan over medium heat and add remaining butter. When butter is foamy, add egg mixture and cook for 5 minutes until edges start to set. Carefully transfer pan to oven. Bake for 15-20 minutes until center is just set. Cut into rounds with a biscuit cutter and serve with potato latke, Gruyère chip, Hollandaise and parsley for garnish. Serves 10

While these soufflés are a bit labor intensive, they make an impressive breakfast or dinner main course. Just remember: the soufflé waits for no one, so be sure to invite punctual guests!

roasted red pepper and
goat cheese soufflé

butter for ramekins

2 cups heavy cream

pinch of salt

fresh ground black pepper

¾ cup flour

6 eggs, separated

1 cup goat cheese

¾ cup chopped roasted red peppers

¼ teaspoon cream of tartar

Preheat oven to 375°. Butter eight 4- or 5-ounce ramekins. In a large saucepan, combine the cream, salt, and pepper and heat over medium-high heat until just simmering. Keep an eye on it as the cream will boil over quickly. Add the flour all at once, whisking constantly to avoid lumps. Turn heat down to low and cook for 2 minutes. Remove from heat; the sauce will be very thick at this point. Add egg yolks one-by-one, stirring between each one to incorporate thoroughly. Add the cheese and peppers, stir to combine and set aside.

In a large clean bowl, beat egg whites until frothy and add cream of tartar. Continue to beat egg whites until stiff, but not dry. Add ⅓ of the egg whites to the soufflé mixture and combine thoroughly. Gently fold the remaining egg whites into the soufflé mixture, taking care not to over mix. A few white streaks are okay.

Spoon the soufflé mixture into the buttered ramekins to ¾ full. To help them rise straight up, flatten the tops and run your thumb around the inside edge to clean off any mixture on the top edge of the ramekin. Put ramekins on a large baking sheet, place in the center of the oven and bake until tops are lightly browned and soufflés have risen, about 20 minutes. Carefully remove from oven and serve immediately as they will fall in a minute or two. Serves 8

LES TROIS ETOILES
57 COURS MIRABEAU
AIX·EN·PROVENCE

There's nothing quite like grits with cheese and bacon. I've just made this dish a bit more sophisticated by turning it into a soufflé.

"southern" soufflé

1 cup quick cook grits

4 cups water

6 large eggs, separated

½ teaspoon salt

1 cup grated cheddar cheese

6 slices cooked, crispy, hickory smoked bacon, diced

¼ cup unsalted butter

¼ teaspoon cream of tartar

Preheat oven to 375°. Butter eight ½ cup ramekins. Combine grits and water in large heavy-bottomed saucepan, cover and cook over medium heat, stirring frequently until very thick, about 12 minutes. Remove from heat. Stir in egg yolks one at a time, then stir in salt, cheese, bacon and butter until combined. Set aside.

With an electric mixer or stick blender, beat egg whites until frothy. Add cream of tartar and beat until whites are stiff, but not dry. Add ⅓ of egg whites to grits and stir to combine. Fold remaining whites into grits, taking care not to over mix. Spoon mixture into buttered ramekins to ¾ full. To help the soufflés rise straight up, flatten the tops and run your thumb around the inside edge of the ramekin to remove any extra batter.

Bake until set and top is lightly browned, about 20 minutes. Serve immediately; soufflés fall after a minute or two. Serves 8

pecan pancakes with
caramelized bananas

1 cup all-purpose flour

½ cup pecans, toasted and finely chopped, plus a few whole toasted pecans for garnish

8 teaspoons vanilla sugar (page 169), divided

4 teaspoons baking powder

1 teaspoon salt

1 cup whole milk

2 eggs

3 tablespoons vegetable oil, separated

8 tablespoons (1 stick) butter, melted and cooled

4 ripe bananas, peeled, cut in half and sliced lengthwise

maple butter sauce (page169)

Place flour, pecans, 4 teaspoons sugar, baking powder, and salt in a large mixing bowl and whisk to combine. Place milk, eggs and 2 tablespoons oil in a small mixing bowl and blend well. Add butter to wet ingredients and stir to combine. Pour wet ingredients into dry and whisk until just combined. Do not over mix. Let mixture rest for 5 minutes.

In a medium bowl, add remaining sugar and bananas and toss to coat. Set aside. Heat ½ teaspoon of oil in cast iron griddle or non-stick skillet over moderate heat until hot. Pour ¼ cup of batter onto skillet for each pancake and cook until bubbles have formed on top and the undersides are golden brown. Turn pancakes over and cook for one minute more. Keep pancakes warm in a 200° oven while you make the bananas. On the same griddle, place bananas with flat sides down and cook until well caramelized, about 3 minutes.

To serve, place a few pancakes on a warm plate, top with caramelized bananas, warm maple butter sauce and whole pecans. Serves about 8

gingerbread waffles

1 cup plus 2 tablespoons all-purpose flour

1 teaspoon baking powder

1 teaspoons baking soda

½ teaspoon salt

½ teaspoon ground cinnamon

1 teaspoon ground ginger

⅛ teaspoon ground cloves

⅛ teaspoon nutmeg

3 tablespoons molasses

1 cup sour cream

1 large egg

3 tablespoons unsalted butter, melted

3 tablespoons whole milk

cooking spray for waffle maker

maple butter sauce (page 169)

vanilla cream (page 171)

Heat a non-stick waffle iron according to the manufacturer's instructions. In a large bowl, whisk together flour, baking powder, baking soda, salt, and spices. In another bowl, whisk together the molasses, sour cream, egg, butter, and milk. Add the wet ingredients to the dry and whisk until just combined. Let stand for about 15 minutes.

Spray the waffle iron with cooking spray, then pour ¼ cup batter per waffle onto hot iron and cook according to instructions. When the waffle stops steaming, it's done. Transfer to a platter and loosely cover with foil to keep warm. Serve with maple butter and vanilla cream. Makes 10 waffles

As a sweet finish to our four-course breakfast, we serve this German pancake cut into little wedges, rolled into crescents and filled with lemon curd or dusted with cinnamon sugar.

liebchen

¼ cup sugar

½ cup sifted flour

½ cup whole milk

2 eggs, room temperature

½ tsp vanilla extract

2 tablespoons butter

¼ cup lemon curd or 2 tablespoons cinnamon sugar

maple butter sauce (page 169)

raspberry coulis (page 167)

Preheat oven to 425°. Combine first 5 ingredients, blending until smooth with a whisk. Heat a 10" cast iron skillet on the stovetop over medium heat and add butter. When butter has melted and is foamy, pour mixture into skillet and cook until edges are set and come up the sides of the skillet, about 2 minutes.

Transfer to oven and bake for 10 minutes. Remove from skillet and spread lemon curd evenly onto middle of Liebchen or dust with cinnamon sugar. Cut into wedges, roll into crescent shapes and serve while hot with maple butter sauce and raspberry coulis. Serves 6

My mom created this recipe and has served it for some 20 years. Naturally, my Mom's portion size is ten times what we serve at the Foster Harris House, but a little goes a long way with this decadent breakfast dessert.

pain du "mom"

1 stick butter plus enough to grease pan

½ cup dark brown sugar

½ cup light brown sugar

1 teaspoon cinnamon

½ teaspoon allspice

8 eggs

¾ cup heavy cream

¾ cup whole milk

½ teaspoon vanilla

12 slices thick cut white bread, crusts removed

raw sugar and cinnamon for dusting

crème anglaise (page 171)

Butter a 9" x 12" baking dish. In a medium saucepan, add butter, sugars, cinnamon and allspice. Heat over medium-low heat, whisking occasionally until melted and combined. Set aside.

In a medium bowl, whisk together the eggs, cream, milk and vanilla and set aside. Lay bread slices in one layer on the bottom of the baking dish and pour half of the egg mixture over the bread. Pour the butter and sugar mixture over the egg-soaked bread, spreading it to cover bread completely. Lay the rest of the bread on top of butter and sugar mixture and top with remaining egg mixture. Refrigerate overnight.

Heat oven to 375°. Remove Pain du Mom from refrigerator 20 minutes before baking. Dust with cinnamon and raw sugar and bake for 35 minutes or until top is brown and puffed up. Let cool for 15 minutes before serving with crème anglaise. Serves 8 to 12

We've adapted this fantastic, simple recipe from Chef Michel Richard as a dramatic looking and tasty breakfast dessert.

cream of wheat crème brûlée
with raspberry coulis

2 cups whole milk

4 large egg yolks

¼ cup quick cook Cream of Wheat

½ cup sugar

2 vanilla beans, split lengthwise and seeds scraped. Save beans for vanilla sugar

pinch of salt

raw sugar

raspberry coulis (page 167)

raspberries and mint for garnish

propane torch

Combine milk, yolks, Cream of Wheat, sugar, vanilla seeds, and salt in a medium saucepan over medium-low heat. Cook, stirring constantly until thickened, about 7 minutes. Remove from heat and pour into a 9 x 9" greased baking dish. Smooth top of crème and cover with plastic wrap pressed directly on surface to prevent skin from forming. Refrigerate for at least 2 hours.

To serve, remove crème from refrigerator and remove plastic wrap. With a 2" biscuit cutter, carefully cut out rounds of the crème and lift them out of the dish with a small offset spatula. Place each round in a shallow bowl or plate and sprinkle tops with a generous amount of raw sugar. Brûlée sugar with torch in slow back-and-forth motion, being careful not to burn sugar. Drizzle raspberry coulis around crème and garnish with a raspberry and mint. Serves 6

When Diane's parents visit, her Dad will wake up early and position himself across from the griddle in the kitchen. He's usually eaten about 30 of these half-dollar-sized pancakes before anyone else has come down to eat!

dad's favorite pancakes

1 cup flour

4 teaspoons vanilla sugar (page 169)

4 teaspoons baking powder

1 teaspoon salt

1 cup whole milk

2 eggs

3 tablespoons vegetable oil, separated

8 tablespoons (1 stick) butter, melted and cooled

shaved dark chocolate

maple butter sauce (page 169)

powdered sugar

mint sprig for garnish

Place flour, vanilla sugar, baking powder, and salt in a large mixing bowl and whisk to combine. Place milk, eggs and 2 tablespoons oil in a small mixing bowl and blend well. Add butter to wet ingredients and stir to combine. Pour wet ingredients into dry and whisk until just combined; do not over mix. Let mixture rest for 5 minutes.

Heat ½ teaspoon of oil in cast iron griddle or non-stick skillet over moderate heat until hot. Pour 1 tablespoon of batter onto skillet for each pancake and cook until bubbles have formed on top and the undersides are golden brown. Turn pancakes over and cook for 1 minute more. Serve hot with shaved chocolate, powdered sugar and maple butter sauce. Garnish with mint.

These pancakes are best when served right off the stove, but can be kept warm in a 180° oven for a few minutes. Makes dozens of half dollar pancakes

chocolate curls

To make chocolate curls, you'll need a vegetable peeler, a clean dish towel and the right chocolate. I've found that *Hershey's Special Dark* chocolate bars work best and taste great. Hold a room temperature chocolate bar with the towel (so you don't melt it with your hands) and shave the edge in long strokes with the peeler. If the chocolate grates instead of rolling into curls, the bar is too cold. When the chocolate temperature is just right, the curls will roll beautifully.

Biscuits are a great addition to bacon and eggs as well as chicken and gravy. This recipe only takes a few minutes and produces lovely, light, flaky biscuits.

cream biscuits

2 cups all-purpose flour

1 tablespoon baking powder

½ teaspoon salt

1¼ cup heavy cream, plus more for brushing

fruit preserves for serving

Preheat oven to 425°. Sift together the flour, baking powder and salt in a cold, large mixing bowl. Stir in cream until dough just starts to form. With floured hands, knead dough in bowl 4 or 5 times.

Turn the dough out onto a cold, floured surface and form into a flat disc about ¾-inch thick. Cut out 2-inch rounds with a biscuit cutter and place on cold, ungreased baking sheet 1½ inches apart. Brush tops with cream and bake for 10-12 minutes, until just golden brown. Makes 12-18 biscuits

Starters

Whoever thought of starting a meal with little tasty finger foods was a genius. Whether you call them hors d'oeuvres, antipasto, meze or tapas, that first little taste before a meal sets the tone for things to come. Or, if you're like us, sometimes the starter serves as the meal itself. An impromptu cocktail hour with friends needs nothing more than some nice cheeses and prosciutto wrapped around just about anything.

These recipes are quick and easy to make; some don't even require you to turn on the stove. Invite some friends over, open some wine and don't even bother with the plates.

The thing that makes or breaks beef tartare is the quality of the meat. Don't skimp on this one; get the best beef tenderloin you can find.

beef tartare on crostini

16 ¼-inch thick slices French bread

¼ cup, plus 2 tablespoons olive oil

2 garlic cloves, 1 whole and 1 minced

2 anchovy fillets

½ cup minced shallots

2 large egg yolks

2 tablespoons Dijon mustard

1½ teaspoons grated orange zest

1 teaspoon Worcestershire sauce

1 pound prime beef tenderloin, chopped

salt and fresh cracked black pepper to taste

¼ cup chopped, fresh, flat-leaf parsley

1 tablespoon white truffle oil

> "I could never bring myself to eat sea urchin until my brother prepared it wrapped in nori and fried in a light tempura batter. I loved it! That's when I realized how important texture is to the overall eating experience."
>
> **– Christina Tompkins, Aberdeen, MD**

Heat oven to 350°. Brush bread slices with olive oil and toast in the oven until lightly browned, about 10 minutes. Remove from the oven and rub with the whole garlic clove. Set crostini aside.

With a mortar and pestle, mash the anchovies, minced garlic and shallots together to make a paste. Transfer paste to a mixing bowl and whisk in egg yolks, mustard, orange zest and Worcestershire sauce. In a slow, steady stream, add the olive oil, whisking constantly to make an emulsion. Add the beef to the mixing bowl and stir with a wooden spoon. Season to taste with salt and pepper.

To serve, spoon some of the tartare on top of each crostini, garnish with parsley and drizzle each with a little truffle oil. Makes 16 crostini

Here in our little town, we have a monthly dinner group we call Tasty Tuesday. The dinner moves from house-to-house and everyone brings part of the meal. One Tasty Tuesday, Diane and I were out of town until six o'clock in the evening with dinner starting at seven. We promised to bring an appetizer, so without much time on my hands, I threw together this shrimp dish. The group decided it needed to be in our cookbook, so here it is.

cilantro garlic shrimp

¼ cup olive oil

3 cloves minced garlic, divided

2 tablespoons dry rub(page 162)

2 pounds large peeled, de-veined, tail on shrimp

salt

small handful cilantro, chopped

1 lime, divided

Heat oven to 375°. In a small saucepan, heat oil, 2 tablespoons garlic and dry rub over low heat for about 3 minutes until oil is hot but not boiling. Set aside. In a large baking pan, add shrimp, remainder of garlic then pour garlic oil over shrimp stirring to coat. Season with salt and bake for about 12 minutes or until shrimp have just turned pink. Remove from oven, add cilantro and the juice of half the lime. Toss to coat and transfer to a serving bowl. Garnish with lime wedges and serve immediately with crusty bread. Serves 8

I prefer Anjou pears for this recipe, but any type of pear will work.

prosciutto-wrapped pear
with maytag cream

8 very thin slices prosciutto

2 medium pears, cored and cut
  into 4 wedges each

3 ounces Maytag blue cheese,
  crumbled (about ½ cup)

¼ cup heavy cream

½ teaspoon finely chopped thyme

freshly ground black pepper

fresh thyme sprigs for garnish

Preheat oven to 425°. Line a baking sheet with parchment paper or aluminum foil.

Place each prosciutto slice flat on a work surface. Place a pear wedge at the end of each slice and roll up, leaving a bit of the pear showing at the top. Transfer the wrapped pear wedges to the baking sheet and bake for about 10 minutes or until the prosciutto is lightly browned and the pear is slightly soft.

While the pears cook, heat the cheese, cream and thyme in a small saucepan over medium heat. Cook until the cheese melts, about 5 minutes, stirring constantly. Season to taste with pepper.

To serve, spoon some Maytag cream into the bottom of a shallow soup bowl and top with a pear wedge. Garnish with thyme sprigs and serve. Serves 8

that can't be any good... but let me have a taste

Sometimes when we try the unexpected, we're richly rewarded. Here are some unusual food combinations shared by our guests:

"Grilled cheese and grape jelly sandwich. Think about it; grapes, cheese and a baguette. All it needs is a glass of Beaujolais!"
  – Jennie Pries, New York, NY

"An appetizer of bittersweet chocolate on steak."
  – Robert Short, Hancock, NH

"Apple and fresh dill pie."
  – Ethan Ham, New York, NY

"Kosher hot dog with grilled pineapple, smoked mozzarella and crushed salt & vinegar potato chips."
  – Anita Lunsford, Miami, FL

"Cantaloupe with a crushed red pepper and salt rub."
  – Steven Goldenberg, Washington, DC

"An Entenmann's chocolate donut topped with Kraft American cheese. It was surprisingly good after I got over the shock of ruining a perfectly good donut."
  – Mike Martin, Fairfax, VA

"There are three worth mentioning: foie gras in beer at Arzak in San Sebastian, Spain, oyster ice cream at Portofino in Stockholm, Sweden, and foie gras ice cream at Oro in Oslo, Norway."
  – Lois and Bob Gajdys, Battle Creek, MD

"Rosemary and grapefruit sorbet."
  – Elizabeth McCarthy, New Canaan, CT

"Grilled cheese with bacon on sour dough raisin bread."
  – Cindy Forcier, Arlington, VA

steamed mussels with dijon mustard and white wine

½ medium onion, chopped

2 tablespoon olive oil

1 cup dry white wine

1 tablespoon Dijon mustard

1 lemon, divided

3 pounds mussels, scrubbed and beards removed

fresh Italian parsley sprigs

In a large pot over medium heat, add oil and cook onion until translucent, about 5 minutes. Stir in wine, mustard and a squeeze of half a lemon. Add mussels and cook covered for about 5 minutes, until mussels have opened, shaking the pot occasionally. Throw away any unopened mussels and transfer the rest to a platter. Top with parsley and lemon wedges.

If you'd like, reduce the steaming liquid over medium-high heat for a minute or two, season with salt and pepper. Serve with the mussels and some crusty bread. Serves 6

"My most unexpected dining experiences always occur in China: from skinned snake, bone in, artfully curled in a bowl to room temperature duck, all parts, including the webbed feet. Once, when seated beside my host who always serves the honored guest, the platter arrived with a conical pile of sea cucumbers in the center, ringed by dozens of deep fried scorpions, tails curled over their backs. As he served me a generous portion, he leaned over to reassure me, "the scorpions are farm raised, Madame." I managed to crunch them down, but when the large glass bowl of live shrimp arrived and the server poured wine on them so they jumped from the bowl, I excused myself to the ladies room and stayed a good long time!"

– Carol Saunders, McLean, VA

For an upscale version of cheese sticks, give this easy recipe a try. Serve them with an interesting dipping sauce such as raspberry chipotle (page 167) or mango chutney (page 162).

black pepper cheddar cheese sticks

1½ cups grated extra-sharp cheddar cheese

1 cup flour plus enough for dusting surface

¾ stick cold butter, cut into 8 pieces

½ teaspoon salt

½ teaspoon coarse ground fresh black pepper

1½ tablespoons milk

Preheat oven to 350°. In a food processor, add cheese, flour, butter, salt and pepper and pulse until blended to a course texture. Add milk and pulse until a ball forms. Don't worry, keep pulsing, a ball will form eventually.

Roll out ball on a floured surface to a thickness of about ¼ inch. Cut into strips about ¼ inch wide and 5 inches long. Transfer to two ungreased baking sheets, spacing strips ½ inch apart. Bake in upper and lower third of the oven for about 12 minutes, rotating pans halfway through baking. Remove when sticks are lightly browned. Store in an airtight container for up to a week. Makes about 60

Here's a recipe for folks that don't like hot wings. These are sweet, salty and sticky... just what you want in a wing.

sticky soy wings

24 chicken wings (about 4 pounds)

1 cup soy sauce

½ cup dry red wine

½ cup brown sugar

½ teaspoon finely minced garlic

1 teaspoon fresh grated ginger

sliced candied ginger for garnish

Preheat oven to 400°. Arrange wings, skin sides down, in a roasting pan large enough to hold them in one layer.

In a small saucepan, heat the next 5 ingredients over medium-low heat, stirring, until sugar is dissolved. Pour evenly over wings. Bake wings in middle of oven for 25 minutes. Turn wings over and bake until cooking liquid is thick and sticky, about 30 to 45 minutes more. Transfer wings to a platter, garnish with ginger and serve. Makes 24 wings

I'm not one for specialty kitchen equipment, but a deli slicer works wonders here. It's the easiest way to get consistently thin slices of cheese. If you don't have a deli slicer, a cheese wire will also work. Be sure to make a bunch of these as they get eaten up very quickly!

gruyère chips

½ pound Gruyère cheese in a block

parchment paper

deli or cheese slicer

Heat oven to 325°. With a deli or cheese slicer, cut Gruyère into ⅛-inch thick slices from the largest part of the block. Stack slices on top of one another and cut the stack diagonally to make triangles. Carefully separate slices and place on a parchment-lined baking sheets with a ½-inch space between slices. Bake for 12 minutes or until golden brown.

Remove from oven and slide parchment paper with cheese onto a cool surface. Gently remove chips when cool with a thin spatula. Store in an airtight container for up to a week. Makes about 50 chips

goat cheese pecan toasts

1 French bread baguette

8 ounces soft, fresh goat cheese

¼ cup honey

½ tablespoon chopped fresh rosemary

½ teaspoon chopped fresh thyme

½ cup chopped toasted pecans

Preheat oven to 350°. Cut 16 - 20 ¼-inch diagonal slices from baguette. Spread some goat cheese on each slice and arrange in a single layer on rimmed baking sheet. Bake until edges are slightly golden and cheese softens, about 10 minutes. Set aside on baking sheet.

Heat honey with herbs in a small bowl in a microwave until warm, about 1 minute. Sprinkle toasts with pecans, then drizzle with honey and serve. Makes 16 - 20 toasts

soups and salads

By the time we check out our guests, get the house ready for new guests, tend to Finn and do a dozen other things, it's well past lunchtime. When we finally sit down to eat, a big salad is more often than not what we'll eat. You can put just about anything on a salad to make it a meal: Grilled shrimp, cranberries, toasted pine nuts, crumbled Paradise Bacon, to name a few. If I made soup the day before, even better. That's the thing I love about soup: make a bunch, put it in the freezer and you have it whenever you want it. As part of a multi-course dinner, I like to serve a small interesting salad or a puréed soup in a demitasse cup for that concentrated shot of flavor.

This creamy soup of sweet carrots and spicy ginger looks striking in a simple white bowl.

carrot ginger soup

½ stick butter

1 medium onion, chopped

2 cloves garlic, minced

1 tablespoon chopped, peeled fresh ginger

1½ pounds medium carrots, peeled and chopped

1 medium sweet potato, peeled and chopped

3 cups chicken stock

⅓ cup heavy cream

2 tablespoons honey

salt and pepper to taste

¼ cup candied ginger, diced

paprika for garnish

In a large heavy pot over medium-high heat, melt butter and sauté onion until translucent, about 5 minutes. Add the garlic and chopped fresh ginger and cook for another minute or two. Add chopped carrots and sweet potato and cook for another minute. Add the chicken stock and bring to a boil. Reduce heat, cover and simmer until vegetables are soft, about 15 to 20 minutes.

Remove from heat and purée soup with a stick blender or in batches in a regular blender. Return soup to the pot and reheat on low. Add heavy cream and honey and season with salt and pepper. At this point, the soup can be cooled to room temperature and refrigerated for a few days or frozen for up to a month. To serve, ladle soup into bowls and garnish with paprika and diced candied ginger. Serves 8

The mild spice and nutty crunch in this hearty, wholesome soup make it one of our favorites on a cold, rainy day.

tomato peanut soup

1 tablespoon peanut oil

1 clove garlic, minced

1 28-ounce can chopped tomatoes

1 6-ounce can tomato paste

½ cup creamy peanut butter

4 cups chicken broth

1 tablespoon balsamic vinegar

¼ teaspoon cayenne pepper

2 teaspoons kosher salt

dill for garnish

¼ cup salted peanuts, coarsely chopped

Heat oil in a large pot over medium heat. Add garlic and cook for 1 minute. Add the tomatoes (do not drain), tomato paste, peanut butter, broth, vinegar, cayenne, and salt and whisk to combine. Bring to a boil. Reduce heat to low, cover, and cook for 20 minutes. Ladle into individual bowls and garnish with the dill and peanuts. Serves 6

under-the-weather favorites

This soup is Diane's favorite when she has the sniffles. When we asked our guests to tell us their favorite comfort foods to soothe a cold, most replied with the gold standard, chicken soup, with tomato soup a close second. Quite a few said Pho, which is a Vietnamese beef noodle soup in a broth with star anise, cinnamon and other fragrant spices. Here are some other under-the-weather favorites our guest shared:

- Glühwein (red wine, heated and spiced with cinnamon sticks, vanilla pods, cloves, citrus and sugar)
- Beef Stroganoff
- Matzah ball soup
- Jjigae (a Korean "stew" seasoned with chili pepper and served boiling hot)
- Congee (rice porridge)
- Chili
- Baked beans
- Hot cocoa
- Spicy Thai food
- Ginger ale with heavily butter popcorn

A nod to Jamie Oliver's friend Bender for finding this recipe in an old book. Quick to make and oh-so good.

chickpea and leek soup

5 large leeks

2 tablespoons butter

2 tablespoons olive oil plus more for garnish

2 cloves of garlic, thinly sliced

1 small peeled potato cut into ½-inch cubes

12 ounces canned chickpeas

3-5 cups chicken broth

½ cup freshly grated Parmesan plus extra for garnish

salt and pepper to taste

Cut off and discard tough green tops of leeks, slice white parts of leeks lengthwise and wash well to remove grit. Roughly chop leeks.

Melt the butter and olive oil over medium-low heat in a heavy pot and add the garlic. Cook for 1 minute, then add the leeks. Once the leeks are translucent, after about 10 minutes, add the potato and chickpeas and cook for 1 or 2 more minutes. Add 3 cups chicken broth and bring to a boil. Reduce heat and simmer for about 15 minutes.

Remove from heat and partially purée with a stick or regular blender. Once you've achieved your desired consistency, add half the cheese and season to taste with salt and pepper. Serve with a drizzle of good olive oil and remaining Parmesan. Serves 6

This soup is easy to prepare, and tastes incrediblly rich and wholesome. Add a loaf of French bread and you have the perfect autumn lunch.

butternut squash soup

½ stick butter

1 medium onion, chopped

1 medium butternut squash, peeled, seeded and chopped

1 large sweet potato, peeled and chopped

4 medium carrots, peeled and chopped

4 cups chicken stock

1 cup heavy cream

2 tablespoons maple syrup

salt and pepper to taste

chives for garnish

In a large heavy pot over medium-high heat, melt butter and add onion, squash, sweet potato and carrots. Cook for about 15 minutes. Add chicken stock, bring to a boil then reduce heat, cover and simmer until vegetables are soft, about 20 to 30 minutes.

Remove from heat and purée soup with a stick blender or in batches in a regular blender. Return soup to the pot and reheat over low. Add heavy cream, maple syrup and season with salt and pepper to taste. This soup can be cooled to room temperature and refrigerated for a few days or frozen for up to a month. To serve, ladle soup into bowls and garnish with chives. Serves 8 to 10

Roasted beets have a wonderfully sweet, earthy flavor. If you have a farmers market nearby, look for yellow, red, purple or even candy-striped beets. They can be roasted, peeled and cut the day before you make this dish.

roasted beet and goat cheese salad

6 medium beets, washed and trimmed

7 ounces goat cheese, preferably in a log shape

¼ cup olive oil

⅓ cup champagne vinegar

1½ teaspoons sugar

2 tablespoons chopped dill

½ cup chopped toasted walnuts

salt and pepper to taste

dill sprigs for garnish

Heat oven to 350°. Wrap washed and trimmed beets loosely in foil and place on a baking sheet. Roast until tender when pierced with a knife, about 1 hour. Remove from oven and let cool. Peel the beets and slice into ½-inch thick discs. To make precise rounds, cut discs with a 1½-inch biscuit cutter. Store beets in an airtight container in the refrigerator until ready to assemble salad.

In a small bowl, whisk together oil, vinegar, sugar and dill. Season with salt and pepper to taste and set aside. Slice goat cheese with a cheese wire into ½-inch thick rounds and set aside.

To assemble, place one beet round in the center of a plate topped with a goat cheese round followed by another beet. Drizzle some dressing around the stack and top with walnuts and a dill sprig. Assemble just before serving so the beet juice doesn't have time to run into the goat cheese. Serves 6

Dinner

Nothing's more satisfying to me than feeding the people I love and dinner is the meal that gathers us all together. Mom always managed to make dinner special, whether it was grilled cheese sandwiches or bracciole. We always dined as a family and enjoyed fresh baked bread from Mirabella's, "under-the-sink" wine, and lots of conversation.

When Diane was about to meet my parents for the first time, I took a moment to prepare her: "When you meet my folks, they'll hug you like a long-lost daughter, and then we'll sit down at the kitchen table to eat and drink for most of the afternoon and evening. Friends and relatives will drop in and squeeze around the table, sitting on mismatched chairs, or standing over the counter to eat chocolate fudge coconut cake or leftover meatballs. The food and wine will just keep coming until the last guest has left."

Diane thought I was exaggerating and wondered if she was up for such a marathon event, but now we laugh about how surprisingly easy it is to spend the better part of the day in a crowded kitchen surrounded by food, wine, and great conversation. Mangia.

brined roast loin of pork

8 allspice berries

8 juniper berries

3 tablespoons black peppercorns

8 cups water

⅓ cup kosher salt

¼ cup sugar

1 tablespoon dried thyme

2 large sprig rosemary

4 whole cloves

1 bay leaf

1 large pork loin

2 tablespoons vegetable oil

cranberry ginger chutney (page 134)

roasted root vegetables (page 130)

With a mortar and pestle, crack allspice, juniper and pepper. If you don't have a mortar and pestle, put berries and peppercorns in a sealable plastic bag and crush with a rolling pin. Add first 10 ingredients to a large pot and stir to combine. Over medium-high heat, bring mixture to a boil until salt and sugar dissolve. Remove from heat and cool completely.

Place pork loin in a large sealable container large enough to hold both the pork and brining liquid. Pour brine over pork and refrigerate at least 8 hours and up to 24 hours.

Heat oven to 375°. Remove pork from brine and drain well. Pat dry with paper towels, taking care not to remove any adhered spices. Heat oil in a large ovenproof skillet over medium-high heat. Sear pork on all sides until nicely browned. Remove from heat, transfer skillet with pork to oven and roast until the internal temperature of the pork is 150°, about 35 minutes. Transfer pork to a serving plate and let it rest for 15 minutes, covered. Slice pork on an angle and serve with chutney and root vegetables. Serves 6 or more

"I haven't eaten beef since the day I locked eyes with a lone cow sticking its head out of the slats of a beef trailer on the highway. Now I just need to pull up next to a pork truck!"

— Delores Nunn, Yorktown, VA

Here's a simple and flavorful short rib dish that pairs perfectly with everything from mashed potatoes to white truffle polenta. A Foster Harris House favorite.

barbecue braised beef short ribs

16 ounces store-bought barbecue sauce (I like *Sweet Baby Ray's*)

¼ cup brown sugar

¼ cup strong brewed coffee

¼ cup bourbon

6 bone-in beef short ribs

¾ teaspoon salt

½ teaspoon fresh ground black pepper

2 tablespoons flour

2 tablespoons vegetable oil

2 cups beef stock

1 cup dry red wine

Heat oven to 325°. In a medium saucepan over medium heat, add the prepared barbecue sauce, brown sugar, coffee and bourbon. Bring to a boil, then reduce heat to low and simmer for about 15 minutes, until slightly thickened. Set aside. Trim ribs of any excess fat and silver-skin. Season with salt and pepper then dredge ribs in flour.

Heat oil over medium-high heat in large stockpot that will fit ribs in a single layer. When oil is just starting to smoke, add ribs and brown on all sides, about 5 minutes per side. When all the ribs have been browned, set them aside and pour off fat from pot. Add sauce, stock and wine, stirring to combine, then add the ribs back to the pot and bring to a boil. Remove from heat, cover, and place pot in the middle of the oven. Braise in the oven for 1½ to 2 hours until ribs are very soft, but still on the bone. Remove from oven and cool in the sauce.

At this point, you can either skim the fat off the top and serve the ribs, or better yet, refrigerate the ribs in the sauce overnight and then remove the solidified fat the next day. Reheat the ribs in the sauce over low heat on the cooktop or in a 250° oven. Serve warm with a little sauce over potatoes, polenta or cauliflower purée (page 131). Serves 6

pan roasted duck breast with balsamic cranberry reduction

¾ cup balsamic vinegar

1 cup cranberry juice

1 shallot, peeled and halved

1 bay leaf

2 sprigs of thyme

8 tablespoons butter

4 duck breast halves, skin on

¼ cup dried cranberries

salt and pepper to taste

Preheat oven to 450°. Place vinegar, juice, shallot, bay leaf and thyme in a small saucepan. Heat over medium heat until boiling, and then reduce heat to low and simmer for 15 minutes until liquid is reduced to ½ cup. Liquid should be slightly syrupy.

With the heat off and the saucepan still on the burner, add the butter, one tablespoon at a time, stirring with a wooden spoon. Continue adding butter bit-by-bit until completely incorporated. Avoid letting the sauce get too hot or cold, as it will separate. Once all the butter is incorporated, remove the shallot and bay leaf and season with salt and pepper. Sauce can be kept warm in a covered bowl in a warm oven or at the back of the stove.

Score the skin of the duck breasts in a crisscross pattern being careful not to cut into the meat. Season the duck with salt and pepper and heat a heavy, large ovenproof skillet over high heat. Add the duck breasts, skin side down, to the dry skillet. Reduce heat to medium and cook until the skin is crispy brown, about 5 minutes. Turn duck over and transfer skillet to the oven and roast for about 10 minutes to 135° for medium-rare. You can use a thermometer to check it. Use tongs to transfer the duck to a plate and let it rest for a few minutes. Cut the duck on an angle into thin slices and serve with cranberry reduction. Serves 4

---

cooking fiasco #4

Our biggest cooking fiasco happened when we were just married. My wife wanted to cook a "gourmet" meal. She decided on roast beef. Neither of us had the slightest idea of how to cook. She put the roast beef in the oven and when the timer went off she looked in the oven and said it didn't look done. I took a look and said that it didn't even look like it was breaking a sweat. We waited another half hour. Nothing. I asked her if she knew what she was doing. She indignantly said she did. We waited another half hour. Nothing. She insisted she had followed the directions in the cookbook to a tee. I asked to see the book. She pointed to the page and said, "See, here's the temperature for medium rare." I looked closely. The temperature she was citing was the meat's INTERNAL temperature for medium rare, not the oven temperature. We had a pretty good laugh." – **Ken Levine, Riverdale, NJ**

For years, I've tried to make my Mom's meatballs the way she does. She adds a pinch of this and a bit of that and I could never get her to give me exact amounts. I finally cornered her and wrote down the recipe step-by-step while she made them. I still can't make them quite the way she does but, really, isn't that how it should be?

[almost] mom's meatballs

1 cup raisins, chopped with hot red wine to cover

2 pounds ground beef, 85% lean

16 crushed Saltine or Ritz crackers, divided

½ teaspoon onion salt

½ teaspoon garlic salt

2 teaspoons finely chopped basil

½ teaspoon cinnamon

1 teaspoon salt

½ teaspoon pepper

¼ cup olive oil

shaved Parmesan

Mom's quick pasta sauce (page 165)

Soak raisins in hot wine for 10 minutes. While raisins soak, blend half the crackers in with the ground beef along with the next 6 ingredients. Add the raisins with the soaking liquid to ground beef mixture. Mix well with your hands and form into 2-inch balls. Roll meatballs in remainder of cracker crumbs to coat.

Heat olive oil in large skillet over medium-high heat and fry meatballs in oil until browned on all sides, about 10 minutes. Transfer to paper towel to drain. Add cooked meatballs to prepared pasta sauce and simmer for 30 minutes. Serve over your favorite pasta with sauce and Parmesan cheese. Serves 6

kiddy meatballs

If you have a tough time getting your kids to eat protein, try adding more raisins to this recipe and making smaller meatballs. Our son Finn gobbles them up!

This pizza dough is great to have on hand for an impromptu meal with friends. Store balls of dough in the freezer, tightly wrapped in plastic and thaw for a few hours before using. The thin, delicate crust is the perfect vehicle for whatever cheeses, meats, and fresh vegetables you have on hand.

pizza dough

¾ cup warm water (105° to 115°)

1 envelope active dry yeast

2 cups all-purpose flour

1 teaspoon sugar

¾ teaspoon salt

3 tablespoons olive oil, plus more for brushing

Pour ¾ cup warm water into small bowl and stir in yeast. Let stand until yeast dissolves, about 5 minutes. Brush large bowl lightly with olive oil. Mix 2 cups flour, sugar and salt in a food processor. Add yeast mixture and 3 tablespoons oil. Process until dough forms a sticky ball. Transfer to a lightly floured surface. Knead dough until smooth, adding more flour if dough is very sticky, about 1 minute. Transfer to oiled bowl. Turn dough in bowl to coat with oil. Cover bowl with plastic wrap and let dough rise in warm, draft-free area until doubled in volume, about 1 hour.

Punch down dough before using. Flatten dough into a disc and continue to push out edges with your fingers, making the disc larger. Use a rolling pin, if needed.

Dough can be made a day ahead. Store in airtight container in refrigerator or wrap in plastic and store in the freezer for up to a month. Makes one large medium-crust pizza or two large thin-crust pizzas

asparagus, prosciutto and fontina pizza

¼ cup olive oil

8 shallots, peeled and thinly sliced

2 tablespoons salt plus a pinch

10 spears asparagus, peeled if very thick

flour for dusting

pizza dough (opposite page)

cornmeal for dusting

1 cup grated Fontina cheese

3 ounces pre-sliced Prosciutto ham, cut
    into ½-inch strips

½ cup grated Parmesan cheese

Heat oven to 450°. In a large skillet, heat 2 tablespoons oil over medium-low heat and add shallots. Cook shallots with a pinch of salt until soft and slightly caramelized, about 15 minutes. Set aside. In a medium pot, boil 4 cups of water with 2 tablespoons salt. Slice asparagus on an angle into ½-inch pieces and blanch in the salted boiling water for 2 minutes. Drain and set aside.

On a floured surface, roll out pizza dough to a thickness of about ¼ inch. Generously dust a large, thin baking sheet with cornmeal. Carefully transfer dough to dusted baking sheet and brush top with olive oil. Spread shallots evenly over top of pizza, then top with Fontina, prosciutto, asparagus and lastly, Parmesan cheese.

Place pizza in the center of the oven and bake until crust is browned and cheese is bubbling, about 15 minutes. Serves 6

beer braised baby backs with bourbon coffee barbecue sauce

16 ounces store-bought barbecue sauce

¼ cup brown sugar

¼ cup strong brewed coffee

¼ cup bourbon

4 pounds baby back ribs

¼ cup dry rub (page 162)

2 12-ounce bottles dark beer

Heat oven to 375°. In a medium sauce pan over medium heat, add the prepared barbecue sauce, brown sugar, coffee and bourbon. Bring to a boil, then reduce heat to low and simmer for about 15 minutes until slightly thickened. Set aside.

Rub both sides of ribs generously with dry rub. Place ribs in a large roasting pan, rib side down, and pour beer around ribs. Cover pan tightly with foil and place in the center of the oven. Roast until ribs are tender, about 1 hour and 15 minutes. Ribs and sauce can be made a day ahead, cooled and covered. Refrigerate separately.

Heat grill to medium-high. Brush ribs with sauce and heat until warmed through and slightly browned, about 10 minutes. Heat the remainder of the sauce over low heat. Brush ribs with a bit more sauce before serving. Slice ribs into racks of 4 and serve with remaining sauce. Serves about 4

cooking fiasco #2

"Many years ago, while doing my residency training, I decided to make Thanksgiving dinner for my family and invited a group of co-workers who didn't have family nearby. The bird cooked beautifully and all the trimmings were ready to go. Imagine my surprise when they told me they were *all* vegetarians! You'd think they might've mentioned that! Anyway, did you know you can turn five-minute couscous into a Thanksgiving feast?"

– Christine Isaacs, Richmond, VA

This is another dish that's been in my family for as long as I can remember. My Mom used straight Smuckers, but I've added a few ingredients to give it a bit more depth.

broiled salmon with orange marmalade and coconut rice

1 cup jasmine rice

1 cup coconut milk

1 cup water

½ teaspoon salt

½ cup orange marmalade

1 teaspoon grated ginger

¼ teaspoon ground chipotle pepper

2 tablespoons bourbon

salt and pepper to taste

4 salmon fillets, preferably Irish salmon

2 tablespoons vegetable oil

black sesame seeds

cilantro sprigs

In a medium saucepan, add rice, coconut milk, water and ½ teaspoon salt. Cover and bring to a boil over medium heat. Reduce heat to low and simmer for 15 to 20 minutes until all the liquid is absorbed. Remove from heat and set aside.

In a small saucepan, add the marmalade, ginger, chipotle pepper, bourbon and a pinch each of salt and pepper. Stir over low heat and simmer for 5 minutes. Place the salmon fillets on a lightly oiled broiling pan and brush with marmalade mixture. Set the oven rack to 6 inches from the broiler and heat to high. Broil salmon for about 5 minutes, until top is starting to brown in places and fish is just cooked through.

Fluff rice with a fork and divide between 4 bowls. Top rice with a salmon fillet and garnish with sesame seeds and cilantro. Serves 4

mediterranean tilapia with israeli couscous

4 pieces skinless tilapia fillet, about 2 pounds total

4 tablespoons butter, divided

1 tablespoon olive oil

½ cup pitted Calamata olives, chopped

1 tablespoon capers, drained

1 tablespoon lemon juice

¼ cup dry white wine

salt and pepper to taste

Israeli couscous, prepared (page 133)

chives for garnish

Cut each fillet lengthwise into two portions. Pat dry and season with salt and pepper. Heat 2 tablespoons butter and 1 tablespoon oil in a 12-inch heavy, nonstick skillet over medium-high heat. Sauté fish in two batches for 3 minutes per side until just cooked through. Transfer to a platter and keep warm, loosely covered with foil. Wipe skillet clean and heat remaining butter over medium heat. Add olives, capers, lemon juice and wine and cook until reduced by half, about 5 minutes.   Season with salt and pepper to taste. Spoon couscous in center of warmed plate, top with a tilapia fillet and sauce with the olive caper butter. Garnish with chopped chives. Serves 4

blackened salmon tacos with smoked paprika aoili

1 cup shredded red cabbage

1 cup shredded green cabbage

2 tablespoons rice wine vinegar

1½ pounds skinless salmon fillets, divided into 8 pieces

salt

2 teaspoons blackened seasoning such as Old Bay

1 tablespoon vegetable oil

8 flour tortillas

avocado salsa (page 37)

smoked paprika aioli (page 165)

juice of 1 lime

In a medium bowl, combine cabbages and vinegar and set aside. Heat a large non-stick skillet over medium-high heat. Season both sides of salmon with salt and blackened seasoning and brush lightly with vegetable oil. Cook salmon undisturbed for 3 minutes until well browned, turn and cook for 2 minutes more, until just cooked through. While salmon cooks, wrap tortillas in paper towel and heat in microwave for 1 minute until warm. Drain cabbage.

To assemble, place a bit of cabbage on tortilla, top with a piece of salmon, one tablespoon salsa, a drizzle of aioli, and a squeeze of lime. Makes 8 tacos

spiced quail with cranberries

8 semi-boneless quail

2 teaspoons dry rub (page 162)

½ teaspoon allspice

juice of 1 lime

½ cup chicken broth

3 tablespoons molasses

½ cup dried cranberries

1 tablespoon minced shallot

1 tablespoon butter

salt and pepper

olive oil

Israeli couscous (page 133) or lime sweet potatoes (page 137)

Prepare Israeli couscous or lime sweet potatoes and keep warm. Wash quail thoroughly and pat dry. Combine dry rub and allspice in a small bowl, then rub on all sides of the quail. Set quail in a baking dish, cover and chill in refrigerator for one hour. While the quail marinates, make the sauce by combining the lime juice, broth, molasses, cranberries and shallot in a small saucepan. Cook over medium heat until sauce is slightly thickened, about 15 minutes. Remove from the heat and whisk in the butter. Season with salt and pepper and keep sauce warm so the sauce doesn't separate.

Set the top oven rack so it's 3 inches away from the broiler, then heat the broiler to high. Brush a broiling pan as well as both sides of the quail lightly with olive oil. Place on the broiling pan and cook for 3 minutes. Turn the quail over and cook for 3 more minutes, until just cooked through.

Place two quail on top of a scoop of couscous or potatoes and drizzle sauce around plate. Serves 4

cashew herb crusted rack of lamb

3 Frenched racks of lamb (8 bones each)

1½ cups finely chopped cashews

¼ cup finely chopped Italian parsley

1 tablespoon finely chopped thyme

2 tablespoon finely chopped mint

2 tablespoon finely chopped rosemary

4 tablespoons olive oil

salt and pepper

Dijon mustard

Heat the oven to 400°. Stir together cashews, the 4 herbs and 2 tablespoons of olive oil. Set aside. Season both sides of the lamb with salt and pepper. Heat the rest of the oil in a skillet over medium-high heat until it's almost smoking. Sear lamb racks on each side until nicely browned, about 5 minutes per side. Once browned, place all 3 racks in a baking dish with the fatty side up. Brush the fatty sides of the racks with mustard, then press the cashew mixture on top, using the mustard as the glue.

Roast the racks in the middle of the oven for about 20 minutes or until the internal temperature of the meat is 138°. This will give you a nice medium-rare lamb chop.

Remove from the oven and let them rest for 15 minutes. Slice between the bones into individual chops. Serves 8

cooking fiasco #3

"My attempt to cook a French veal dish for my wife resulted in a new formula for leather wallets."

– R. Jean Vallieres, Alexandria, VA

117

There's nothing more welcoming than the smell of a chicken roasting in the oven and this dish will fill your kitchen with wonderful aromas. Use whatever herbs you have on hand, the fresher the better.

lemon herb garlic roasted chicken

1 roasting chicken, 3–4 pounds

6 tablespoons butter

salt and pepper

1 cup chopped fresh herbs, plus a handful of whole herbs

1 lemon, quartered

1 head of garlic

2 bay leaves

olive oil

Heat the oven to 400°. Thoroughly wash chicken inside and out and pat dry. Season the inside of the chicken generously with salt and pepper.
Blend the butter with a pinch of salt and pepper and the chopped herbs into a paste. Set aside.

With your fingers, carefully separate the skin from the breast meat, taking care not to tear the skin. You want to form 2 pockets as far towards the legs and thighs as possible. Carefully push the herb butter into the pockets, spreading it evenly under the skin.

Smash the garlic with your hand to break up the cloves and stuff it all inside the cavity, along with all the lemon, whole herbs and bay leaves.

Place chicken in a roasting pan, brush with oil and roast in the center of the oven for about 1 hour or until the juices run clear when a thigh is pierced with a fork. If the skin starts to brown too much, tent the chicken loosely with foil.
Serves 6

Here are our two favorite ways to prepare a steak. One for cooking outside when the weather's good, the other for inside when it's not so great. Either way, you end up with a great steak.

the steak

2 (1½-inches thick each) New York strip or boneless rib eye steaks

2 tablespoon olive oil

2 tablespoons dry rub (page 162)

salt and pepper

Season both sides of the steaks generously with salt and pepper and a generous amount of dry rub. Let stand covered at room temperature for 30 minutes.

For cooking outside

Heat your gas grill for 15 minutes on the highest setting with the cover closed. For charcoal, the grill is ready when the coals are ash covered and glowing.

Brush steaks with olive oil. Grill steaks with grill lid up for 8 minutes, undisturbed. Keep a squirt bottle with water handy for flare-ups. Turn steaks and grill for an additional 6 minutes for medium rare. Remove from grill, tent loosely with foil and let rest for 10 minutes before serving.

For cooking inside

Heat the oven to 500°. Heat a cast iron skillet or grill pan over medium-high heat until very hot.

Brush steaks with olive oil. Grill steaks undisturbed for 8 minutes. Turn steaks and place in the center of the oven and cook for 6 minutes more for medium rare. Remove from oven, transfer steaks to a plate and tent loosely with foil. Let them rest for 10 minutes before serving.

Serves 2

grilled ribeye on lime sweet potatoes with sautéed morels

lime sweet potatoes (see page 137)

2 tablespoons olive oil, divided

2 1-inch thick ribeye steaks

6 tablespoons butter, divided

1 shallot minced

24 fresh morels (about 1 pound), washed well, patted dry, and trimmed, or 1 ounce dried
morels, soaked in warm water, reserving ½ cup soaking liquid

½ cup red wine

2 tablespoons balsamic vinegar

2 tablespoons chopped green onion, divided

salt and pepper

Prepare lime sweet potatoes, cover and keep warm. Heat gas grill for 15 minutes on the highest setting with the cover closed or heat a grill pan over high heat on the stove. Brush steaks with 1 tablespoon olive oil and generously season both sides with salt and pepper. Grill steaks for 8 minutes without disturbing them. Turn steaks and grill for an additional 6 minutes for medium rare. Remove from grill, tent loosely with foil and let rest.

While steaks are grilling, place large pan over medium heat and add olive oil and 2 tablespoons butter. Add shallot and cook for 1 minute. Add morels and cook until edges start to crisp, about 10 minutes. Remove mushrooms to a bowl, cover and keep warm. Increase heat to medium-high and deglaze pan with wine, cooking for a minute or so. Add vinegar and cook until reduced by half. Remove from heat and add remainder of butter piece-by-piece, stirring to incorporate after each piece. Season sauce to taste and keep warm so butter does not separate.

Slice steaks on an angle into 1-inch wide strips. Place some potatoes in the center of a plate, top with steak strips and morels. Drizzle sauce around plate and garnish with green onions. Serves 4

asparagus risotto

1 quart chicken stock

1 pound asparagus

4 tablespoons butter, divided

4 tablespoons olive oil, divided

1 medium onion, chopped

2 cups Arborio rice

½ cup dry white wine

½ grated Parmesan cheese, plus more for garnish

salt and pepper

Trim woody ends off asparagus and peel if thick. Save top 2 – 3 inches of spears and chop remaining stalks. Heat the chicken stock to a simmer. Cook asparagus in chicken stock for 5 – 8 minutes, until al dente. Remove from stock and refresh in cold water. Set aside. Return stock to a simmer.

In a large pot, heat 2 tablespoons butter and 2 tablespoons oil over medium-low heat. Cook onion until translucent, about 10 minutes. Add rice and stir to coat. Add wine and cook until all the liquid is absorbed.

Add one ladleful of the stock to the rice, stirring constantly until all the liquid is absorbed. Continue adding the stock this way until the rice is thick and creamy. Test the rice to see that it's soft, but with a hint of bite in the center of the grain. Once the rice is ready, add the chopped asparagus, ½ cup of cheese, the remainder of butter and oil and stir to combine. Season to taste with salt and pepper. Spoon risotto into warmed shallow bowls and top with asparagus spears and shaved Parmesan. Serves 4

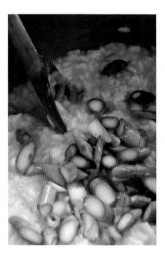

This is one of the quickest dinner dishes you can prepare. Most people serve it over pasta, but for a change, I serve it with basmati rice which soaks up all the wonderful garlicky, buttery sauce.

cilantro shrimp scampi

prepared basmati rice

¼ cup olive oil

1 pound large peeled, de-veined, tail-on shrimp

4 tablespoons minced garlic

pinch of cayenne pepper

½ cup dry white wine

2 tablespoons lime juice

salt and pepper to taste

2 tablespoons chopped, fresh cilantro

6 tablespoons butter

Prepare rice as directed on packaging and keep warm. While rice cooks, heat oil in a large, heavy skillet over medium-high heat until hot. Sauté shrimp, turning over once, until just cooked through, about 2 minutes. Transfer with a slotted spoon to a large bowl. To the same pan with remaining oil, add garlic, cayenne, wine, lime juice, salt and pepper. Cook over high heat, stirring occasionally until slightly reduced, about 1 minute. Add butter to skillet, stirring until melted, and then add shrimp.

To serve, place a few large tablespoons of rice on a large plate and top with some shrimp and a drizzle of the pan sauce. Garnish with a sprig of cilantro and serve immediately with some crusty bread. Serves 4

service winner

"When we were traveling in Lerici, Italy, the hotel staff recommended we go next door to the local tennis courts for dinner. Because of the language barrier, we weren't sure we had heard them right when we walked up the hill and found nothing more than a few old plastic tables and chairs. My husband asked the closest tennis pro about getting a meal, and he only replied, "Sit down." We asked to see a menu but were told simply, "Sit." We tried to order red wine and were kindly told "no" and given a glass of white instead. After five minutes, two huge steaming bowls of "Frutti De Mare" appeared (perfectly paired with the crisp white local wine of course), and we found ourselves eating the best meal of our lives while listening to locals play tennis and watching the sunset over the Ligurian Sea." **– Anita Lunsford, Miami, FL**

Side Dishes

Side dishes are the supporting cast to your roast turkey or grilled ribeye, but sometimes end up getting more attention than the main dish. On more than one occasion, I've been to a potluck dinner where a side dish has rightly stolen the show.

Many of these easy side dish recipes can be made well ahead and reheated just before dinner. Some can even stand alone as simple meals all by themselves.

roasted root vegetables

2 large sweet potatoes, cut into 1-inch cubes

2 large fennel bulbs, cored, cut into wedges

1 large celery root (celeriac), peeled, cut into 1-inch cubes

4 large carrots, peeled and cut into 1-inch pieces

4 large parsnips, peeled and cut into 1-inch pieces

10 large garlic cloves, peeled

10 shallots, peeled

2 large sprigs of thyme

2 large sprigs of rosemary

salt and pepper

½ cup olive oil

Preheat oven to 375°. Combine vegetables, garlic, shallots and herbs in large bowl. Sprinkle generously with salt and pepper. Add olive oil and toss to coat. Spread out vegetables on two large rimmed baking sheets. Roast vegetables until tender, stirring occasionally, about 1 hour.

Vegetables can be made 4 hours ahead, cooled and covered at room temperature. Reheat in a 250° oven. Serves 8

Cauliflower purée is a great dish for experimenting. Enhance it with herbs, blue cheese, or bacon bits. Once you start making this side dish, it'll be a permanent fixture in your repertoire.

cauliflower purée

1 head cauliflower, 2 to 2½ pounds

3 tablespoons unsalted butter

¼ cup heavy cream

1 teaspoon salt

¼ teaspoon ground black pepper

pinch of nutmeg

Heat about 1 inch of water to boiling in the base of a steamer pot. Wash and trim the cauliflower, then cut out the stem in a cone-shape to detach the florets. Separate the florets into similar small sizes and add to steamer basket. Cover and steam until just tender. You want the cauliflower to have a bit of resistance when pierced with a knife. Place the steamed cauliflower into a food processor along with the butter, cream, salt, pepper and nutmeg. Process to a smooth purée. Check seasonings and serve hot.
Serves 4

stumbling upon greatness

"On a short trip to Vienna last November, my wife Minh and I were walking through the old district looking for a place to eat. We were jet-lagged, it was cold and rainy, and we weren't looking for anything special. A cozy place with white tablecloths caught our eye. We came in through what turned out to be the back door, sopping wet, and asked for a table from the maitre'd, who had a long mutton chop mustache and wore an elaborate red velvet vest. Despite not having reservations, we were escorted to a central table. Only when we saw the menu did we have any idea where we were; Zum Schwarzen Kameel, ("At the Black Camel") is apparently a well-known food landmark in Austria, established in 1618 and once a favorite of Beethoven. The meal that followed was fantastic, highlighted by an off-the-menu pasta in a white truffle sauce which the waiter couldn't permit us to miss, since the local truffles had just been harvested. He was right, and we remember that dish and that meal as the best dining surprise of our lives."

– Chris Dymond, Chevy Chase, MD

Israeli couscous is a larger grain pasta than the quick-cook couscous most people know. It's usually toasted in a little butter or oil before adding any water or broth.

israeli couscous with cranberries, almonds and thyme

4 tablespoons butter

1 shallot, minced

1 cup Israeli couscous

¼ cup dry white wine

2 cups chicken broth

½ cup dried cranberries

1 teaspoon fresh thyme leaves

½ cup sliced toasted almonds

½ teaspoon fresh lemon juice

salt and pepper

In a medium saucepan, heat butter over medium heat until foam subsides. Add shallot and cook, stirring often until translucent, taking care not to let it brown. Add couscous and cook, stirring often until toasted and aromatic. Add wine and cook until almost all the liquid has evaporated.

Add broth, cranberries and thyme and cook covered for 15 minutes or until the liquid has been absorbed and couscous is al dente. Remove from heat and stir in almonds and lemon juice. Season to taste with salt and pepper. Serves 4-6

cranberry-ginger chutney

1½ cups sugar

¾ cup apple cider

⅓ cup apple cider vinegar

1 12-ounce bag fresh or frozen cranberries
(about 3 cups)

1 large Bosc pear, peeled, cored, cut into ½-inch
cubes

¼ cup finely chopped peeled fresh ginger

¼ teaspoon dried crushed red pepper

salt and pepper to taste

Stir the sugar, cider, and vinegar in a heavy, large saucepan over medium-high heat until the sugar dissolves. Add the remaining ingredients and bring to a boil. Reduce heat to medium and simmer until chutney thickens, stirring occasionally, about 20 minutes. Season with salt and pepper and transfer to bowl and allow to cool to room temperature. Serve right away or cover and chill. Chutney can be made 3 days ahead stored in the refrigerator. Serves 8 - 10

coconut rice

1½ cups coconut milk

¾ cup chicken stock

1 cup jasmine rice

¾ teaspoon salt

In a small saucepan, bring coconut milk, chicken stock, and salt to a boil and stir in rice. Reduce heat to low and simmer rice, covered, until most of liquid is absorbed, about 20 minutes. Remove pan from heat and let rice stand, covered, about 5 minutes. Serves 6

potato latkes

1 pound Russet or Yukon Gold potatoes

1 large egg, lightly beaten

½ teaspoon salt plus a pinch

4 tablespoons melted butter

¾ cup vegetable oil

Peel potatoes and coarsely grate by hand, transferring to a large colander. Rinse grated potatoes under cold water until water runs clear. Squeeze excess water from potatoes, then spread grated potatoes on a kitchen towel and roll up, twisting ends in opposite directions. Twist towel tightly to wring out as much liquid as possible. Transfer potatoes to a bowl and stir in egg, ½ teaspoon salt and butter.

Heat ¾ cup oil in a 12-inch nonstick skillet over medium-high heat until hot, but not smoking, about 400°. Spoon 2 tablespoons of potato mixture into 3-inch round mold or biscuit cutter. Flatten potatoes in mold with the back of a spoon and lift off mold. Repeat with remaining potato mixture. With an offset spatula, gently place latkes into oil and cook until undersides are browned, about 5 minutes. Turn latkes over and cook until undersides are browned, about 5 minutes more. Transfer to paper towels to drain and season with a pinch of salt. Add more oil to skillet as needed. Keep latkes warm on a wire rack set in a shallow baking pan in oven.

Latkes may be made up to 8 hours ahead and reheated on a rack set over a baking sheet in a 350° oven for about 5 minutes. Makes about 8 latkes

Although the combination of sweet potatoes and lime may sound strange, this dish is fantastic and is a refreshing change from the ordinary.

roasted sweet potatoes with lime syrup

3½ pounds sweet potatoes, peeled and cut into ½-inch cubes (10 cups)

½ stick (¼ cup) unsalted butter, melted

¾ teaspoon salt

½ teaspoon black pepper

¼ cup water

2 tablespoons sugar

1 tablespoon fresh lime juice

½ teaspoon finely grated fresh lime zest

2 tablespoons finely chopped fresh chives

Put oven racks in upper and lower thirds of oven and preheat oven to 450°. Toss potatoes with butter, salt, and pepper in a bowl until well coated, then spread in a single layer in 2 shallow baking pans (15 x 10 x 1 inch) and roast, uncovered, switching position of pans halfway through roasting, until potatoes are tender and undersides are browned, 15 to 20 minutes total.

While potatoes roast, bring water, sugar, and lime juice to a boil in a small saucepan, stirring until sugar is dissolved, then simmer until reduced to about 3 tablespoons, 3 to 4 minutes. Toss potatoes with syrup and zest in a large bowl. Garnish with chives and serve immediately.

Potatoes can be roasted and syrup made one day ahead (without tossing together). Chill separately in airtight containers. Reheat potatoes in a single roasting pan in a 300° oven, and heat syrup in a small saucepan until hot. Toss potatoes with syrup and zest. Garnish with chives and serve warm. Serves 6

One of our favorite restaurants in Southern California, Bandera, makes an unbelievable skillet cornbread. Once after dinner, we asked the manager for the recipe, but he said he couldn't share it. A year or so after we moved to Virginia, I decided to call them and make one last plea, explaining that we couldn't bear being 3000 miles away from our favorite cornbread. The person who answered the phone didn't divulge his identity and wouldn't give me the recipe outright, but when I suggested ingredients, he'd say things like, "there might be that much cornmeal... maybe a little more" or, "you could use kernel corn, if that was all you had." Needless to say, I never got the exact recipe, but after a number of iterations, I think it's pretty close.

almost famous skillet corn bread

1½ sticks butter plus 3 tablespoons for skillet

1 cup sugar

1 can cream corn

3 eggs

1½ cups cheddar cheese

½ to 1 teaspoon minced pickled jalapeño peppers

1 cup yellow stone ground corn meal

1 cup flour

1 teaspoon baking powder

½ teaspoon salt

Place large cast iron skillet in oven and heat to 325°. In a large bowl, add butter and sugar and beat until creamy. Add cream corn, eggs, cheese and jalapeño to butter mixture blending well.

In another large bowl, add cornmeal, flour, baking powder and salt. Whisk to combine. Add the wet ingredients to the dry ingredients, folding together until blended, but taking care not to over mix. A couple of dry lumps are okay.

Remove skillet from oven, add reserved butter, swirling to coat bottom of skillet, then pour in batter. Bake for 45 - 55 minutes or until a cake tester inserted into the center of the bread comes out clean. Serve warm with honey. Serves 8

dessert

Dessert can turn an ordinary meal into a fantastic dining event. Guests may not remember what they had for the first course, but chances are they'll remember the last. Here at the Foster Harris House, dessert is such an important part of our eating ritual that we serve a sweet finish with breakfast everyday.

Now, dessert need not be a big production. Our favorite evening treat is a small bowl of vanilla bean ice cream with chocolate chips. But sometimes you want something special for that dinner you worked on all day: Imagine a chocolate soufflé to end a great meal or a cheesecake that'll make people close their eyes and sigh.

There are few things in life that gratify people as instantly as dessert. Let's make the world a happier place!

basic crêpes

1 cup flour
¼ teaspoon salt
2 large eggs
1¼ cups whole milk
butter, melted

Whisk together flour and salt in a large bowl and set aside. In a smaller bowl, whisk eggs and milk together. Whisk egg mixture into flour mixture, blending well. The mixture should be about the thickness of heavy cream. If it's too thick, add a little more milk. It's best to let the batter stand for 30 minutes or so, but if time does not allow, no worries.

Heat an 8-inch diameter nonstick skillet over medium-high heat. Brush with melted butter. Pour enough batter into skillet to coat bottom and swirl to coat evenly. Cook until the top appears dry, loosening sides of crêpe with a spatula, about 45 seconds. Turn and cook until brown spots appear on the second side, about 30 seconds. Turn crêpe out onto parchment paper and continue making crêpes in the same manner.

Crêpes will keep in the refrigerator, wrapped tightly, for 5 days or in the freezer for a month. Makes 12 crêpes

brandied strawberry crêpes

6 tablespoons butter

1 quart strawberries, washed and sliced

2 tablespoons sugar

2 teaspoons lemon juice

¼ cup brandy

2 cups vanilla ice cream

4 prepared crêpes (page 142)

raw sugar for dusting

Heat butter in a large nonstick pan over medium heat until bubbles have subsided. Add strawberries, sugar and lemon juice and cook until bubbling. Carefully add brandy and flame to burn off alcohol. Remove from heat and set aside.

Lay crêpes on a flat work surface and place ½ cup ice cream in center of crêpe. Wrap crêpe around ice cream and place on serving plate. Repeat with remaining crêpes.

Pour ¼ of the strawberry mixture over each crêpe and dust with raw sugar. Serve immediately. Serves 4

---

cooking fiasco #5

We were preparing cheese fondue for a Christmas family gathering in Ohio and my husband had filled the burner too high with denatured alcohol. When he ignited it, the fuel spilled onto the tray underneath and flames began to dance everywhere. Alarmed, he threw open the sliding doors and chucked the entire fondue pot into a two-foot high snow bank! The fire was quelled, and we started anew with great relief, family laughter and much more wine! – **Barbara Mabee, Cleveland, OH**

This recipe makes about 8 servings when prepared in 5-ounce ramekins. You can also make them in ovenproof coffee mugs. The dark chocolate truffles really make these a rich and decadent way to end a meal. The soufflés can be covered and refrigerated up to 24 hours before baking.

chocolate soufflé

8 ounces semisweet or bittersweet chocolate, chopped

6 tablespoons butter

2 tablespoons coffee

6 eggs, separated and at room temperature

¼ teaspoon cream of tartar

½ cup sugar

8 dark chocolate truffles (Lindt, Godiva...)

crème anglaise (page 171)

Heat the oven to 375°. Butter the ramekins or mugs well and place in the freezer for 10 minutes. Remove from freezer and butter again. Sugar the insides, dumping out the extra. Refrigerate until you're ready to use them.

In a double boiler over simmering water, combine chocolate, butter and coffee, stirring until melted and combined. Let mixture cool, then whisk in egg yolks. Beat the egg whites in a clean, large bowl until frothy. Add the cream of tartar and beat until soft peaks form. Gradually beat in sugar until the mixture is glossy, but not too dry. Stir ⅓ of the egg whites into the chocolate mixture to lighten it, and then gently fold in the rest.

Divide the batter equally among the ramekins and push a truffle down into the middle of each one. Smooth the tops and then run your thumb around the inside edge to help the soufflé rise straight up. Bake for 20 minutes until they have risen and are dry on top. Serve immediately with crème anglaise. Serves 8

This is, by far, the easiest and best cheesecake recipe I've ever come across. The ginger-snap crust and spiked vanilla peach sauce put it over the top.

gingersnap cheesecake with spiked vanilla peach sauce

1 gingersnap crust (page 150)

24 ounces cream cheese, room temperature

4 large eggs

2 teaspoon vanilla, divided

1 cup sugar, plus 1 tablespoon for topping

16 ounces sour cream

spiked vanilla peach sauce (page 168)

Make crumb crust as directed. Preheat oven to 350°. Beat cream cheese with an electric mixer until fluffy. Add eggs, one at a time, then 1 teaspoon vanilla and 1 cup sugar, beating on low speed until each ingredient is incorporated, scraping down bowl between additions.

Put springform pan with crust in a shallow baking pan. Pour filling into crust and bake in baking pan (to catch drips) in middle of oven for 45 - 55 minutes, or until cake is set within 3 inches of edge, but center is still slightly wobbly when pan is gently shaken. Let stand in baking pan on a rack 5 minutes. Leave oven on.

To make the topping, stir together sour cream, 1 tablespoon sugar, and 1 teaspoon vanilla. Drop spoonfuls of topping around edge of cake and spread gently over center, smoothing evenly. Bake cake with topping 10 minutes.

Run a knife around top edge of cake to loosen and cool completely in springform pan on rack. Chill cake, loosely covered, at least 6 hours. Remove side from pan and transfer cake to a plate. Bring to room temperature before serving with peach sauce. Serves 12

If you had to eat the same three-course dinner for the rest of your life, what would it be?

"Mediterranean chicken with roasted potatoes, spinach gratin and orange-almond cream cake." **– Delores Nunn, Yorktown, VA**

"Grilled medium-rare filet mignon, a loaf of Swiss bread with butter, and a bowl of Starbucks java chip ice cream." **– Marlene Champagne, Alexandria, VA**

"Leg of lamb, lima beans, mashed potatoes and blueberries for dessert." **– Nancy Boyce, Hancock, NH**

"Maki sushi, a seasonal fruit salad and a Reuben sandwich." **– Ethan Ham, New York, NY**

"Vegetable soup, a cheeseburger with fries, and a bowl of chocolate-vanilla swirl ice cream." **– Ian Bower, Sewickley, PA**

"Thai spring rolls, Beef Stroganoff, and rocky road ice cream." **– Mike Martin, Fairfax, VA**

"Stuffed mushroom pastries, roasted chicken, mashed potatoes, corn-on-the-cob, tomatoes and lemon sponge pie." **– Elizabeth Evans, Mountainside, NJ**

"Homemade chili with a salad and a Pepsi." **– Romaine Woods, Odenton, MD**

Use this crumb crust for cheesecake or key lime pie.

ginger snap crust

9-inch springform pan

5 tablespoons butter, melted plus some for pan

1½ cups finely ground gingersnaps

⅓ cup sugar

⅛ teaspoon salt

Invert the bottom of the springform pan to make the cake easier to remove. Place a piece of parchment paper on the bottom before you close it in the pan. Trim off the excess paper. Butter bottom and sides of pan.

Mix all ingredients in a medium bowl, then press crust mixture into bottom and up sides of pan. Make the crust a uniform thickness as best you can. Run your thumb around the top edge to even out the crust. Refrigerate until ready to use. Makes 1 crust

continued...

"New England clam chowder, rib eye steak, and apple pie" **– Christopher Traci, Arlington, VA**

"Vichyssoise, chicken salad, and coconut cream pie." **– Jim Seely, San Francisco, CA**

"Fried chicken, butter beans over white rice, fresh tomato slices, and a big hunk of vanilla cake with chocolate icing." **– Leslie Conroy, Vienna, VA**

"Sauteéd foie gras with a light raspberry sauce, a rare rib eye with a loaded baked potato, yellow squash and zucchini cooked with onions and bacon fat and a warm vanilla soufflé with a small scoop of homemade vanilla ice cream." **– Gregg Tate, Arlington, VA**

"Nachos, sea bass and scallops, and vanilla pudding with crusted graham crackers."
– Chaya Merrill, Clifton, VA

"Chicken kabobs with garlic yogurt, basmati rice, broiled tomatoes and Ben & Jerry's cinnamon bun ice cream." **– Missy Eng, Arlington, VA**

"A salad, a burrito, an orange, and nuts." **– Deirdre Begley, Reston, VA**

Here's the easiest dessert you'll every make short of scooping ice cream into a bowl. Chances are you already have all the ingredients in your pantry.

dump cake with ice cream

½ box of white or yellow cake mix

1 can of your favorite pie filling (cherry, blueberry…)

1 stick of butter, melted

vanilla ice cream

Heat the oven to 400° and butter a 9 x 12 inch baking dish. Pour the pie filling into the baking dish and spread evenly. Dust the dry cake mix over the pie filling and then drizzle the melted butter on top. Bake for 40 minutes or until the top is nicely browned. Remove from the oven and spoon into serving bowls. Top with a scoop of vanilla ice cream.
Serves 6

covert delights

Everyone has favorite foods that may not rank very high in terms of sophistication. Some may remind us of our childhood (like macaroni and cheese), some may herald in a holiday (like marshmallow-topped sweet potatoes) and still others are just plain good (like McDonald's French Fries). We asked our guests, at the risk of embarrassing themselves in front of their epicurean friends, to admit to a few secret indulgences. Here they are:

"Tuna noodle casserole made with Campbell's cream of mushroom soup."
– Jennie Pries, New York, NY

"Li'l Debbie Peanut Butter Cookies." **– R. Jean Vallieres, Alexandria, VA**

"I could eat a whole box of 'Dots' candy in one sitting." **– Elizabeth Evans, Mountainside, NJ**

"Fried bologna sandwiches." **– Molly Traci, Arlington, VA**

"My Nana's homemade mush, congealed in a loaf, fried in butter with scrapple and served with real maple syrup. I wish she were still alive to make it for me." **– Carol Saunders, McLean, VA**

"Creamed chipped beef on toast." **– Jim Seely, San Francisco, CA**

"Frozen, store-bought fish sticks with a dipping sauce of Miracle Whip and ketchup."
– Michael Sutherland, Fredericksburg, VA

"White Castle Hamburgers." **– Marietta Horne, Cranford, NJ**

"Hot dip made with Velveeta, tomatoes and Jimmy Dean sausage. Ho Hos are also excellent."
– Leslie Conroy, Vienna, VA

toasted pecan cream cheese ice cream

6 ounces cream cheese, room temperature

1 cup milk

1 tablespoon fresh lemon juice

¾ cup sugar

⅛ teaspoon salt

¾ cup toasted, chopped pecans

¾ cup heavy cream

In a blender, mix cream cheese, milk, lemon juice, sugar and salt until smooth. Transfer to a bowl and stir in pecans and heavy cream. Process the cream cheese mixture in an ice cream maker according to the instructions. Transfer the soft ice cream to an airtight container and put in freezer to harden for at least 2 hours. Makes 1 quart

ginger cream cheese ice cream

8 ounces cream cheese, room temperature

1 cup milk

1 tablespoon fresh lemon juice

¾ cup sugar

⅛ teaspoon salt

¾ candied ginger, chopped

½ cup heavy cream

In a blender, mix cream cheese, milk, lemon juice, sugar, and salt until smooth. Transfer to a bowl and stir in ginger and heavy cream. Process the cream cheese mixture in an ice cream maker according to the instructions. Transfer the soft ice cream to an airtight container and put in freezer to harden for at least 2 hours. Makes 1 quart

blackberry frangipane tarts

5 tablespoons cold butter, chopped

⅓ cup powdered sugar

¾ cup ground almonds

2 egg yolks

½ teaspoon vanilla extract

1 sheet puff pastry

1 egg, whisked

10 ounces blackberries, cut in half

raw sugar for dusting

vanilla ice cream

In a food processor, combine first 5 ingredients and blend until smooth. Transfer to a bowl and chill in the refrigerator until cold. Frangipane can be made two days ahead, stored in a sealed container in the refrigerator.

Heat the oven to 400°. Lay the puff pastry sheet on a cutting board and, with a sharp knife or square cutter, cut out 3 x 3-inch squares. With a sharp knife, score a border ½ inch inside the outer edge of each square. Prick the center of each square with a fork and brush the entire square with egg.

Spread the frangipane inside the border of each square, ¼-inch thick, and top with blackberries, cut side down. Dust with sugar and place on an ungreased baking sheet. Bake for 20 minutes or until pastry is golden brown. Serve with a spoonful of vanilla ice cream, sprinkled with raw sugar. Serves 6

A simple cookie is the perfect accompaniment to hot coffee or tea.

simple shortbread cookies

8 ounces butter

2 cups flour

½ cup sugar

pinch of salt

With a mixer, cream butter and sugar. Gradually add flour and salt until dough forms. Transfer dough to a floured work surface and roll into a 2-inch diameter log. Wrap log in plastic wrap and chill in the refrigerator for 30 minutes.

Heat the oven to 275°. Remove log from refrigerator and slice into ¼-inch thick cookies. Place on ungreased cookie sheet and bake for 35 minutes or until blonde colored (not brown). Cool on rack. Cookies will keep in a sealed container for a week. Makes 18 cookies

sauces, rubs, & sugars

A good steak becomes a great steak with the right dry rub and a drizzle of pan sauce. Store bought brownies are fine, but aren't they even better with a swirl of crème anglaise?

Coulis, aioli, cream -- whatever you want to call it -- a dish isn't quite finished until it has that last little touch of sauce. These are a few of our favorite finishing touches.

Use this dry rub on chicken, meat or veggies. It makes an excellent dry marinade and seasoning.

dry rub

3 tablespoons fresh ground pepper

3 tablespoons salt

3 tablespoons dark brown sugar

½ teaspoon chipotle pepper powder

3 tablespoons paprika

½ teaspoon cayenne pepper

½ teaspoon garlic powder

½ teaspoon onion powder

¼ teaspoon cinnamon

Mix all ingredients together well and store in an airtight container. Lasts for months in a cool, dry place. Makes about ¾ cup

mango chutney

⅓ cup mango chutney (with large chunks chopped)

3 tablespoons water

1 tablespoon light or dark brown sugar

2 tablespoons yellow or brown mustard

1 tablespoon cider vinegar

In a small bowl, stir all ingredients together until well blended. Refrigerate until ready to use. Makes ½ cup

chipotle cream sauce

1 teaspoon adobo sauce (liquid from a can of chipotles en adobo)

4 tablespoons butter

2 tablespoons flour

1 cup heavy cream

1 cup whole milk

½ teaspoon dry rub (page 162)

salt and pepper to taste

In a 2-quart sauce pan, heat butter over medium heat until foam subsides. Add flour all at once and cook for 30 seconds, whisking constantly. Add remaining ingredients and whisk often until sauce comes to a boil. Reduce heat to low and simmer for 15 minutes, whisking occasionally until sauce is thickened.

To make a very smooth sauce, strain through a fine mesh sieve into another saucepan and heat over very low heat, stirring constantly. Season to taste with salt and pepper. Makes 2 cups

Any fresh herbs can be used to flavor this easy Hollandaise. Just replace the basil with what you have fresh on hand. It's also great without any herbs at all.

basil hollandaise

4 egg yolks

1-2 teaspoons fresh lemon juice, divided

8 tablespoons butter

salt and pepper to taste

10 basil leaves

In a blender, add yolks and ½ teaspoon lemon juice. In a small saucepan, melt butter over medium-high heat until bubbling. With cover in place, turn blender on high and blend for 30 seconds. Remove center cap on lid and slowly pour hot, bubbling butter into egg yolk mixture. Stop blender, scrape down sides and add basil. Pulse to chop basil. Season with salt, pepper and remaining lemon juice to taste. Makes about a cup

This is our go-to sauce for pork, beef and game. It can be modified to compliment most any dish; just replace the wine with pomegranate juice, Madeira, port, cranberry juice, or whatever you like.

balsamic red wine butter sauce

¾ cup balsamic vinegar

1 cup red wine

1 shallot, peeled and halved

8 tablespoons butter

salt and pepper to taste

Place vinegar, wine and shallot in a small saucepan. Heat over medium heat until boiling, then reduce heat to low and simmer for 15 minutes until liquid is reduced to a half cup. Liquid should be slightly syrupy.

With the heat on very low, move the sauce pan almost completely off burner and add butter, a tablespoon at a time, stirring with a wooden spoon. Continue adding butter bit-by-bit until completely incorporated. Don't let the sauce get too hot or cold, as it will separate. Once all the butter is incorporated, remove the shallot and season with salt and pepper.

Sauce can be kept warm in a covered bowl in a warm oven or at the back of the stove. If the sauce should separate, reheat over low heat, add 1 tablespoon cream and stir to combine. Makes about a cup

smoked paprika aioli

½ cup mayonnaise

2 teaspoons smoked paprika

2 tablespoons white wine vinegar

2 teaspoons lime juice

hefty pinch salt

hefty pinch white pepper

Combine all ingredients in a small bowl. Use right away or aioli can be stored in the refrigerator in a sealed container for up to a week. Makes about ¾ cup

While I love chopping a pile of tomatoes and cooking them down for 4 or 5 hours, my Mom's recipe yields fantastic results in about 30 minutes. It makes the kitchen smell wonderful and can't be beat when you need a sauce right away.

mom's quick pasta sauce

2 tablespoons olive oil

1 large sweet onion, chopped

1 large clove garlic, minced

2 28-ounce cans crushed tomatoes

1 6-ounce can tomato paste

½ cup red wine, more if you like

4 tablespoons brown sugar

large pinch of cinnamon

1 tablespoon dried basil or ¼ cup chopped fresh basil

salt and pepper

In a large sauté pan, heat oil over medium heat and cook onion until translucent, about 6 minutes. Add garlic and cook for 1 minute more. Add chopped tomatoes, tomato paste, wine, brown sugar, cinnamon and dried basil (if you're using it dried), and bring to a boil. Reduce heat to low, cover and simmer for about 20 minutes, stirring occasionally. Season to taste with salt and pepper. If you're using fresh basil, add it just before serving the sauce. Serves 8

raspberry coulis

2½ cups fresh or frozen raspberries

¼ cup sugar

1 teaspoon fresh lemon juice, or to taste

In a medium saucepan, heat raspberries and sugar over low heat until berries start to break down and sugar dissolves. Remove from heat and purée mixture in a blender or food processor. Pour mixture through a fine sieve into a bowl, pressing on solids. Add lemon juice to taste. Coulis will keep 3 days covered in the refrigerator.

We use this sauce for our Paradise Bacon, but it's also delicious on cream cheese with crackers, pork loin, or chicken wings.

raspberry chipotle sauce

1 tablespoon olive oil

½ cup small diced onion

2 teaspoons minced garlic

2 teaspoons chipotles en adobo, chopped

2 pints fresh or frozen raspberries, rinsed

½ cup raspberry vinegar

¾ cup sugar

½ teaspoon salt

Place oil in a medium saucepan over medium heat. Add the onions and cook, stirring until soft and slightly caramelized, about 5 minutes. Add the garlic to the pan and cook for 1 minute. Add the chipotles and cook, stirring continuously, for one minute. Add the raspberries and cook until soft, about 3 minutes. Add the vinegar and stir to deglaze the pan. Add the sugar and salt, and bring to a boil.

Reduce the heat to medium and simmer until thickened and reduced by half, 10 to 15 minutes, stirring gently to break up raspberries. Remove from the heat and cool before using. Store in the refrigerator in an airtight container for up to a week.

This is an easy sauce for anything chocolate or bread pudding-like. It's even great in coffee!

vanilla sauce

2 cups heavy cream

1 vanilla bean

2 teaspoons confectioners' sugar

Place heavy cream and sugar in a 2-quart sauce pan. Slice vanilla bean lengthwise and scrape out seeds with the tip of a knife. Add vanilla seeds and pods to cream mixture and heat over medium heat until boiling, stirring frequently. Reduce heat to low and simmer for 15 minutes, until liquid has slightly thickened.

Remove bean pods from sauce and strain through a fine mesh strainer into a clean bowl. Use immediately or cool completely and store in an airtight container in the refrigerator for up to a week.

spiked vanilla peach sauce

13 ounces peach preserves

1 vanilla bean, split and seeds scraped

¼ cup bourbon

In a small saucepan over low heat, add all ingredients, including vanilla bean, and cook for about 5 minutes until simmering. Remove from heat, then remove vanilla bean and strain sauce through a medium sieve, pressing on solids.

Use right away or store cooled sauce in sealed container in refrigerator for up to 2 weeks. Makes 13 ounces

Maple butter sauce is perfect for pancakes and waffles, but it's also a great topping for ice cream, granola, baked apples, and other desserts.

maple butter sauce

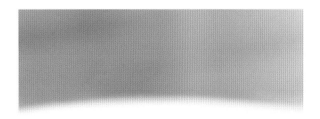

1 cup pure maple syrup

8 tablespoons (1 stick) of butter

½ teaspoon ground allspice

½ teaspoon ground cinnamon

Place all ingredients in a 2-quart sauce-pan and heat over medium heat until boiling. Reduce heat to low and simmer for 15 minutes until liquid has slightly thickened.

Use immediately or cool completely and store in an airtight container in the refrigerator for up to a week.

This is a great way to use vanilla beans that have been scraped of their seeds; just be sure not to use pods that have been soaked or cooked.

vanilla sugar

2 cups granulated sugar

3 or more used vanilla beans

Place sugar and vanilla beans in an airtight container and store in a cool dry place. Sugar will absorb vanilla flavor in a few days. As sugar is used, simply add more sugar and vanilla beans. Makes 2 cups

Crème anglaise is the be-all-end-all sauce for many decadent desserts. I like to serve it with our Pain du Mom and chocolate soufflé. Drizzle some over brownies and ice cream. Heck, eat it right off the spoon!

crème anglaise

1 cup of milk

1 cup of heavy cream

⅓ cup of sugar

1 vanilla bean split and seeds scraped

5 large egg yolks

medium mixing bowl, set over ice

In a medium saucepan, heat milk, cream, half of the sugar, vanilla bean and seeds over medium heat to a simmer. Remove pan from the heat and set aside.

In a small bowl, whisk the remaining sugar and egg yolks to blend. Gradually whisk in about ⅓ of the cream mixture to temper the yolks, then transfer the contents of the bowl back to the saucepan. Heat the mixture over low heat, stirring constantly with a wooden spoon until the cream coats the back of the spoon.

Once thickened, pour contents into the bowl set over ice and cool, stirring occasionally until chilled. Strain mixture through a fine mesh sieve and refrigerate until needed. Sauce can be made up to 5 days ahead. Makes 2½ cups. Serves 8 to 10

vanilla cream

1 cup heavy cream

1 teaspoon vanilla extract

2 teaspoons confectioners' sugar

1 cup sour cream

In a large bowl, combine cream, vanilla and sugar. Vigorously whisk mixture until soft peaks form. Gently fold in sour cream. Store in refrigerator for up to 2 days. Makes 2 cups

appendix

guest picks for best hole-in-the-wall restaurants

Diane and I still dream about the blackened salmon tacos at our favorite hole-in-the-wall restaurant, La Sirena Grill, in Laguna Beach, California. The tiny building on Mermaid Street, downtown -- but decidedly off the beaten path -- seats about eight and is mostly a take-out counter for hungry locals looking for cheap, healthy, authentic Mexican food.

While writing this book, I looked up La Sirena on the web (www.lasirenagrill.com) and was stunned to see a slick, full-blown, corporate-looking site. They now have four locations and it looks like they're franchising. The prices are still great and the food may be, too, but it's no longer our little secret.

We asked our guests to share their favorite hole-in-the-wall restaurants and we hope to visit some of them in our travels. But we won't be surprised if a few have lost a little of that scruffy, unsophisticated charm. And that's okay. After all, 30 years ago, The Inn at Little Washington was one of those little local gems; We're so glad the secret's out!

[Restaurants are listed in order of proximity to Washington, DC]

Pho 75, Arlington, VA, 703-525-7355

"A real pho shop serves nothing but pho, and has communal seating at long benches. People from all walks of life and all backgrounds come together to enjoy the soup. We used to go every weekend, and our children have been eating pho since they've had teeth." – *Chris Dymond, Chevy Chase, MD*

The Forrest Inn, Arlington, VA, (703) 536-7660

"...like falling into a divey bar/restaurant/grill in a small Georgia city. The southern accents, the music on the jukebox, the longneck Buds at 6am in front of the regular patrons all make this a true gem (or horror, depending on your point-of-view). They make the most amazing $4.95 full breakfast (eggs, hash browns, breakfast pork, toast, coffee) that you've ever had, and if you add a Bloody Mary or a Screwdriver (both strong and delicious), you're set for the morning (just don't go back to work...)." – *Gregg and Susan Tate, Arlington, VA*

Ray's the Steaks, Arlington, VA, (703) 841-0001

"It's pretty well-known in the area, but it's so small, I'd say it's a hole-in-the-wall. The beef is incredibly high quality, and because of the no-frills décor and family ownership, they keep their prices very reasonable. The table gets unlimited mashed potatoes and creamed spinach to share. You can't beat that." – *Missy Eng, Arlington, VA*

Rustico Restaurant and Bar, Alexandria, VA, www.rusticorestaurant.com

"Awesome selection of beers, and great stone oven pizzas" – *R. Jean Vallieres, Alexandria, VA*

Vienna Inn, Vienna, VA, www.viennainn.com

"The Vienna Inn has been around forever. They serve up the best chili cheese dogs around and have great beer on tap. You can also buy kegs there. It's a famous local dive and you'll see everything from rusty pick-ups to Mercedes in the parking lot. You walk in and nobody cares who or what you are. They also make you pour your own coffee." – *Leslie Conroy, Vienna, VA*

Ice House Café, Herndon, VA, www.icehousecafe.com

"It's a cozy place with great food (especially the raw oysters), at an affordable price, and wonderful live music." – *Anjali Sharma, Ashburn, VA*

Galway Bay, Annapolis MD, www.galway2006.com

"The food is good and the atmosphere can't be beat; it's in a very old building." – *Joanne Kassmann, Pasadena, MD*

Andy Nelson's Barbeque, Cockeysville, MD, www.andynelsonsbbq.com

"Located on a busy highway, the building is a small, red, shed-like structure with a giant pink pig on the roof. Figurines and collectibles of pigs adorn the walls and tables. But they have the best barbeque on the East Coast! From mouth-watering pulled pork sandwiches and baby back ribs to homemade baked beans and coleslaw, their menu appeals to adults and kids alike. And their signature barbeque sauce is the best!" – *Christina and Matt Tompkins, Aberdeen, MD*

Pierce's Pitt Bar-b-que, Williamsburg, VA, www.pierces.com

"Brings back great memories of law school. Has the best pulled pork sandwiches and hush puppies. It's always crowded, so I know I'm not alone." – *Pam Arluk, Arlington, VA*

Hobby's Deli, Newark, NJ, www.hobbysdeli.com

"Hobby's is an old Jewish deli/restaurant that's been in Newark forever. They have the BEST hot pastrami in the world: HUGE portions!! All the waitresses have worked there for at least 30 years; a definite find and a "must eat" if in the Newark area (tough area, though)." – *Nancy Boyce, Hancock, NH*

Café Paris, Cranford, NJ, (908) 276-8030

"Healthy french food, warm atmosphere, friendly owner." – *Elizabeth Evans, Mountainside, NJ*

Kanoyama, New York, NY, www.kanoyama.com

"Understated, no pretense, just incredible ingredients and hospitable service." – *Jennie Pries, New York, NY*

Caracas Arepa Bar, New York, NY, www.caracasarepabar.com

"Amazing Venezuelan sandwiches." – *Ethan Ham, New York, NY*

Totonno's, New York, NY, www.totonnos.com

"It's a basic pizza and salad place (they also serve pasta). The décor is Christmas lights year round, the waitstaff sometimes speak English, the plates are old; all of it adds to the authentic feel of the place, open since 1924. The pizza is perfect, paper thin, with just the right amount of zesty-and-sweet tomato sauce and cheese. The mozzarella must be homemade; it has a wonderful salty flavor. The salads are also equally good, simple but fresh. It's far from fancy and there are many "famous" pizza places in Manhattan, but on any given night, families and couples pack this unpretentious restaurant for some of the best pizza around." – *Emily Hammann, Cockeyesille MD*

The Sycamore Drive-In Restaurant, Bethel, CT, www.sycamoredrivein.com
"A classic 1950s diner (not because it was designed that way, but because it has stayed that way forever). They have exceptional burgers with hand ground beef mixed with chopped onions. They flatten the burger on the grill so the edges are lacy and crispy. I have to make a trek to Bethel at least quarterly to feed the need!" – *Elizabeth McCarthy, New Canaan, CT*

Vietnam Restaurant, Ithaca, NY, www.vietnam-restaurant.biz
There's a great little Vietnamese restaurant in the town where I went to college. They make the best roast duck on rice! -- *Wei-Fang Lin, Fairfax, VA*

Loveless Café, Nashville, TN, www.lovelesscafe.com

"The Loveless used to be a motel that sits at the entrance to the Natchez Trace Parkway, which is a beautiful road that runs from Nashville to Natchez, MS. Breakfast is their specialty, particularly their biscuits and jam!" – *Rebecca Mullen, Alexandria, VA*

(continued)

guest picks for best hole-in-the-wall restaurants
(continued)

Zingerman's Delicatessen, Ann Arbor, MI, www.zingermansdeli.com

"It's not exactly unknown (actually, it's pretty famous), but they serve the world's best corned beef sandwiches. I know; I've tried to find a deli that beats them. They match lean corned beef with amazing Swiss cheese and funky coleslaw. On top of that, they have the most wonderful selection of cheeses, breads, oils, spices, desserts and all types of other goodies from all over the world. It's a foodie's dream." – *Steven Goldenberg, Washington, DC*

Flo's Hot Dogs, Cape Neddick, ME, www.floshotdogs.com

"Flo's is a true hole-in-the-wall, because it's not so much of a restaurant as it is an indoor hot dog stand. It's a red painted converted trailer that has sat on the side of Route 1 for about 50 years. There's no place to sit inside the "restaurant" and they're only open weekdays from 11am to 2pm. The line is always out the door, because they're locally famous and make hot dogs in an old steam hot dog machine that only fits about 25 dogs at a time. It's not a great place to go if you're tall or claustrophobic or you don't like hot dogs, because all they serve is hot dogs, chips and soda. But as you can only imagine, the hot dogs must be something if folks are willing to tolerate standing in line for over an hour while getting feasted on by some of Maine's other frequent diners, the mosquitoes. Flo's became famous with a secret sauce which is an onion based, sweet and tangy concoction that's unlike anything you've ever put on a hot dog before. It's an addictive mix. " – *Mike Martin, Fairfax, VA*

Chris Madrid's, San Antonio, TX, www.chrismadrids.com

"It's fairly big, but if you drove by it, you'd never know it was a restaurant. They have wonderful juicy burgers, the specialty being the Tostada Burger dripping with refried beans and a mound of cheddar cheese. And the fries are greasy and downright good." -- *Maggie Feldt, Bethesda, MD*

Kokomo Café, Los Angeles, CA, www.kokomocafe.com

"While you enjoy fresh, hot apple spice cake with your morning coffee, you can hear every language being spoken around you, smell the scents of 40 food booths mingling together, and watch the fresh produce being inspected and scrutinized by the locals."
– *Anita Lunsford, Miami, FL*

Klöeter ("Chicken Ranch"), Möelsheim, Germany, www.kloeter-moelsheim.de

"Having a meal there was akin to dying and going straight to heaven. For a mere 18 Deutsch Marks (about $9 U.S. dollars), you could eat a Rahm Schnitzel (veal in cream sauce) the size of a small pizza. There's not a culture on the planet that compares to Germans when it comes to making gravies and sauces. Side dishes included hefty bowls of salad and pommes frites (French fries). Top it all off with a large, cold Eichbaum beer and a shot of schnapps for dessert; David Copperfield couldn't come close to levitating like that." -- *Marlene Champagne, Alexandria, VA*

Grapes on the vine at Rappahannock Cellars in Hume, VA

resources

We have many tools at our disposal these days to help with recipes, meal ideas, and ingredients. Included below are some of the people and places that have inspired me. To everyone associated with each one, a sincere thank you.

Books

Culinary Institute of America, *The Professional Chef*, 7th Edition, Wiley, New York, 2002

Granger, Bill, *Bill's Open Kitchen*, Murdoch, Australia, 2003

Keller, Thomas, *The French Laundry Cookbook*, Artisan, New York, 1999

King Arthur, *The King Arthur Flour Baker's Companion*, Countryman, Vermont, 2003

O'Connell, Patrick, *The Inn at Little Washington Cookbook*, Random House, New York, 1996

O'Connell, Patrick, *Patrick O'Connell's Refined American Cuisine*, Bulfinch, New York, 2004

Phaidon Press, *The Silver Spoon*, Phaidon, New York, 2005

Reichl, Ruth, *The Gourmet Cookbook*, Houghton Mifflin, New York, 2004

Richard, Michel, *Happy in the Kitchen*, Artisan, New York, 2006

Fine Ingredients

The Chef's Warehouse, Hanover, Maryland

The Farm at Sunnyside, Washington, Virginia

Jenkins Orchard, Woodville, Virginia

M. Slavin and Sons, Arlington, Virginia

Roy's Orchard, Sperryville, Virginia

Sperryville Corner Store, Sperryville, Virginia

Waterpenny Farm, Sperryville, Virginia

Wegmans, Gainesville, Virginia

index